THE GOODNESS OF GOD

DAVID HOPE

All Scripture quotations are from the King James Version of the Bible.

All rights reserved. Written permission must be secured from the publisher to use or reproduce any part of this book, except for brief quotations in critical reviews or articles.

Copyright © 2008 by David Hope

ISBN 0-9772194-2-9

ISBN13 978-0-9772194-2-1

Library of Congress Control Number: 2008939341

Printed in the United States of America.

RevMedia Publishing
PO Box 5172
Kingwood, TX 77325

A division of Revelation Ministries

www.revministries.com
www.revmedianetwork.com
www.revmediapublishing.com
www.revmediatv.com

CONTENTS

Preface		7
Chapter 1	Location, Location, Location	9
Chapter 2	The Hiding Place	23
Chapter 3	God's Plan for Man	33
Chapter 4	Que Sera, Sera, Whatever Will Be Will Be	49
Chapter 5	God Has Not Forgotten You	57
Chapter 6	God Wants You Healed	61
Chapter 7	What About Tribulations?	79
Chapter 8	How to Recover What the Devil Has Stolen	97
Chapter 9	Changing Our Thinking	107
Chapter 10	Introduction to the Book of Job	117
Chapter 11	The Trouble with Job's Thinking	123
Conclusion		145

Preface

God has good thoughts and plans for each one of us. If we will trust him completely he will lead us to everything good.

"No good thing will he withhold from them that walk uprightly" (Ps. 84:11b).

Many times, we may have to walk through difficulties, but if we trust God, we will always end up with the blessings of God.

"Better is the end of a thing than the beginning" (Eccl. 7:8a).

Our real trouble comes when we go our own way and go to a plan of our own choosing rather than the plan that God has for us. The knowledge of the goodness of God that you will find described in this book will cause your thinking to change so that you'll make better decisions. The best decision you can make is to move into the hiding place of the arms of a loving God.

We have to stop thinking like man and start thinking like God. God thinks differently from man:

Our Natural Mind Says	God Says
I'll believe it when I see it.	You'll see it when you believe it.
You have to live before you can die.	You have to die before you can live.

Our Natural Mind Says	God Says
If I had it, I'd give.	If you'd give, you'd have it.
Do	Done

I pray that after you read this book, you will change your thinking so that you will do what is right in the mind of God instead of what is right in the mind of man.

"There is a way that seemeth right to man, but the end there of are the ways of death" (Prov. 14:12).

Chapter 1

Location, Location, Location

As you read this book about the goodness of God, I want you to expect God to do something good for you. As Oral Roberts used to say, "Something good is going to happen to you." In order that you can experience the reality of God's goodness in the real world of today, let's start with some basics so that we can walk together in our full inheritance as children of God. If you are not already born again, it is my prayer that as you read this book you will desire the good things of the Kingdom of God and give your life to Jesus.

"Fear not, little flock; for it is your Father's good pleasure to give you the kingdom" (Luke 12:32).

Did you know that we can do something to put ourselves in a position to receive the blessings of God? I'm sure you have heard that the three most important things in real estate are location, location and location. Location is not only important to us in the natural realm, but it is of vital importance in the spiritual realm as well. The Bible says that the Old Testament writings are for examples to us.

"Moreover, brethren, I would not that ye should be ignorant, how that all our fathers were under the cloud, and all passed through the sea; And were baptized unto Moses in the cloud and in the sea: Now all these things happened unto them for ensamples: and they are written for our admonition, upon whom the ends of the world are come" (1 Cor. 10:1–2, 11).

These examples are natural pictures, given so we can understand spiritual principles. For everything that happens in the natural occurs first in the spirit. God has a spiritual location he wants us to be in so that he can prosper, bless, and protect us in the natural realm. Here are some examples given to us so that we can understand how to receive the goodness of God:

"Now the LORD had said unto Abram, Get thee out of thy country, and from thy kindred, and from thy father's house, unto a land that I will shew thee: And I will make of thee a great nation, and I will bless thee, and make thy name great: and thou shalt be a blessing: And I will bless them that bless thee, and curse him that curseth thee: and in thee shall all families of the earth be blessed" (Gen. 12:1–3).

In order to receive all the blessings that God had for him, Abram had to change locations. He had to get in the place that God desired for him in order to walk in the wonderful destiny and promises that God so desperately wanted to give him. Remember, this is a natural example to show us there is a spiritual location where God wants us to dwell.

The Book of Jonah tells us a story about an Old Testament prophet who wanted to do what seemed right to him rather than what seemed right to God. He decided to work his own plan, and it brought great trouble into his life. He thought that there was something wrong with God's thinking, and yet all along it was Jonah's thinking that was all wrong. We have to accept the fact that if our thinking disagrees with God, that God is right and we are wrong. We are the ones who have to change our thinking, not God.

Jonah made the biggest mistake a man can make. We are told in Jonah 1:10 that he fled from the presence of the Lord. We should always run *to* God, not away from God, *especially* when we have messed up. There is nowhere else that we might find mercy like the mercy God will give us.

"For thou, Lord, art good, and ready to forgive; and plenteous in mercy unto all them that call upon thee" (Ps. 86:5).

"For the Lord is good; his mercy is everlasting; and his truth endureth to all generations" (Ps. 100:5).

"It is of the LORD's mercies that we are not consumed, because his compassions fail not. They are new every morning: great is thy faithfulness" (Lam. 3:22–23).

So Jonah's troubles began, and he eventually found himself in the stomach of a great fish. No matter how bad our situation is, it is never too late to change our thinking to obey and call upon the Lord.

"But I will sacrifice unto thee with the voice of thanksgiving; I will pay that that I have vowed. Salvation is of the Lord. And the Lord spake unto the fish, and it vomited out Jonah upon the dry land" (Jonah 2:9–10).

Whenever we call on the name of the Lord with a thankful heart, God will cause us to be vomited right out of our trouble. It is interesting to note that Jonah received the mercy and deliverance of God, even though his mind still needed some renewing. Even through the end of the Book of Jonah, God is still straightening out Jonah's thinking.

God responded to the heart change in Jonah, even though Jonah still had a long way to go in his thinking. God will meet you right where you are at the point of your need. Don't be afraid of God and run from God, for he is thinking good things about you.

"For I know the thoughts that I think towards you, saith the Lord, thoughts of peace, and not of evil, to give you an expected end" (Jer. 29:11).

Jonah did not get out of his troubles until he was willing to go to the location that God would use to bless him. Things started to change for the better in his life when he decided to go to Ninevah, the location that God had chosen.
Mephibosheth, son of Jonathan, needed to change his thinking or die. We all do. David, who became king, cut a blood covenant with Jonathan. This covenant included their seed as they stated the terms of their covenant.

"And Jonathan said to David, Go in peace, for as much as we have sworn both of us in the name of the LORD, saying, the LORD be between you and me, and between my seed and thy seed for ever. And he arose and departed: and Jonathan went into the city" (1 Sam. 20:42).

This was a picture of our relationship with Jesus as we enter into a blood covenant with him when we receive him as our Lord and our Savior.

Mephibosheth was five years old when news of the deaths of his father and grandfather, Jonathan and Saul, reached him. Mephibosheth was taught to fear David and was told to run from

King David because David wanted to kill him and destroy him. He believed bad teaching about the king, which proclaimed that King David would kill all of Saul's remaining family and all who were loyal to Saul. Of course, David didn't intend to do this, but Saul's family believed that this is how David thought.

The Bible gives us an account in 2 Samuel 4:4 where Mephibosheth's nurse drops the young boy as she flees from the sound of the horses of King David's men. She takes the child and "escapes" to Lodebar, a desert wilderness, to hide out. Mephibosheth becomes lame in both feet as a result of his fall.

Mephibosheth's heart hardens against David, his two lame feet continually testifying that David hates him and wants to kill him. Mephibosheth grows up like a runaway slave in fear of David. He doesn't know the truth that he is in covenant with the king through his father, Jonathan. Meanwhile, David longs to show kindness to any of Saul's family because he is in covenant with Jonathan. "And David said, Is there yet any that is left of the house of Saul, that I may shew him kindness for Jonathan's sake?" (2 Sam. 9:1).

The king finally gets the chance to be faithful to his blood covenant.

"And the king said, Is there not yet any of the house of Saul, that I may shew the kindness of God unto him? And Ziba said unto the king, Jonathan hath yet a son, which is lame on his feet. And the king said unto him, Where is he? And Ziba said unto the king, Behold, he is in the house of Machir, the son of Ammiel, in Lo-debar. Then king David sent, and fetched him out of the house of Machir, the son of Ammiel from Lo-debar.

Now when Mephibosheth, the son of Jonathan, the son of Saul, was come into David, he fell on his face, and did reverence. And David said, Mephibosheth. And he answered, Behold thy servant! And David said unto him, Fear not: for I will surely shew thee kindness for Jonathan thy father's sake, and will restore thee all the land of Saul thy father; and thou shalt eat bread at my table continually. And he bowed himself, and said, What is thy servant, that thou shouldest look upon such a dead dog as I am? Then the king called to Ziba, Saul's servant, and said unto him, I have given unto thy master's son all that pertained to Saul and to all his house. Thou therefore, and thy sons, and thy servants, shall till the land for him, and thou shalt bring in the fruits, that thy master's son may have food to eat: but Mephibosheth thy master's son shall eat bread always at my table. Now Ziba had 15 sons and 20 servants. Then said Ziba unto the king, According to all that my lord the king hath commanded his servant, so shall thy servant do. As for Mephibosheth, said the king, he shall eat at my table, as one of the king's sons. And Mephibosheth had a young son, whose name was Micah. And all that dwelt in the house of Ziba were servants unto Mephibosheth. So Mephibosheth dwelt in Jerusalem: for he did eat continually at the king's table; and was lame on both feet" (2 Sam. 9:3–13).

In verse 8, Mephibosheth said, "What is thy servant, that thou shouldest look upon such a dead dog as I am?" Why did Mephibosheth say that? He was overwhelmed in his emotions because David did not want to kill him, as he always had believed; instead, the king wanted to bless him. Many people today have heard bad teaching about Jesus our king. They have heard that God is out to get them. When a servant of the king comes to them and tells them that the king loves them and wants to bring them in to his family and bless them, then they too may get overwhelmed like Mephibosheth.

This is why Mephibosheth referred to himself as a dead dog. What he was really saying was this:
"How could you want me? You must know the things that I have said about you and how I have blamed you for my lame feet. I know it wasn't your fault. The accident resulted from someone else's unjustified fear and wrong thinking about you. I listened to all the lies about you, and I believed them. I told people how I hated you. I made jokes about you. I cursed you. I swore that I would never serve you. I've hated you and I've blamed you for everything bad that has ever happened to me. Instead of living in the wilderness in lack, I could have been in the king's palace under your protection. I continually rejected you, yet you kept loving me and wanting me with a desire to do good to me. You want me just the way I am, even with all my flaws. I'm not worthy of this love and compassion. I don't deserve your mercy and forgiveness."

David's response is a picture of God's response to us. This is what King David was really saying to Mephibosheth:

"I know you don't deserve my unconditional and everlasting love. There is nothing you can do to make up for your thoughts and actions. I'm not doing this because you deserve it but because blood has been shed. I'm doing this because I have entered into an everlasting blood covenant with Jonathan, your father. Here are the terms of the covenant: I will bless you. I will restore all your land. I will forgive all your wrongs against me. My house is your house. You will live here with me at the king's palace.

I will be a father to you and adopt you as my own son." Now, Mephibosheth must choose because he has a free will. He can turn down the covenant. Mephibosheth, however, makes the right choice. King Jesus is saying the same thing to you today. He wants you to be in blood covenant with him. You don't deserve it, but blood has been shed so that whosoever will can enter in. God has given us free will. We must choose to accept this free gift. God is offering to forgive all your wrongs, bless you, and adopt you as his very own son or daughter. I pray you make the right choice as Mephibosheth did.

As long as Mephibosheth was in the place of his own choosing, he was in a wilderness, in lack, and considered a nobody. As soon as he decided to go to the place of blessing of God's choosing, he immediately was in the king's palace. He was in abundance and was a somebody—a child of the king. Location is very important to you and me.

The life of Elijah also shows us the importance of the right location. During a drought, he had to go to a place of God's choosing. While he was in the place that God had chosen for him, he had plenty of water and the ravens fed him supernaturally. God is a God who sees ahead and makes provision. When the brook dried up, God told him to go to Zarephath, a new location, for the Lord had already commanded a widow woman to sustain him there. Upon the act of obedience to go to the right location, there was provision, and supernatural miracles resumed, culminating with the raising of the widow's son from the dead.

The best example of all about changing locations to walk in the blessings of God is the example of the children of Israel in Egypt. While in Egypt, they were in bondage under the taskmasters of Pharaoh. They cried out to God and God heard their cries. He sent them a messenger named Moses. What was Moses' message? His message was this: It's time to change locations. It's time to go to a land that God had given them that flowed with milk and honey.

"And they spake unto all the company of the children of Israel, saying, the land, which we passed through to search it, is an exceeding good land. If the LORD delight in us, then he will bring us into this land, and give it us; a land which floweth with milk and honey" (Num. 14:7–8).

The blessing was for the people, but the blessing was on the land—the special place of God.

"For the land, wither thou goest in to possess it, is not as the land of Egypt, from whence you came out, where thou sowedst thy seed, and wateredst it with thy foot, as a garden of herbs: But the land, wither ye go to possess it, is a land of hills and valleys, and drinketh water of the rain of heaven: A land which the LORD thy God careth for: the eyes of the LORD thy God are always upon it, from the beginning of the year even unto the end of the year" (Deut. 11:10–12).

We have to make a decision to move, just as the people in the Old Testament decided to move. But most of the children of Israel did not make it. They kept thinking the old way. We have to change from the old way of thinking (like men) to the kingdom way of thinking as a child of the king. If we do, we will move from a place of danger, found in this world, to a place the world has never known—the special place of blessing and protection called the hiding place of God.

The message of changing locations is not limited to the Old Testament. There are some examples in the New Testament as well. Let's look at the prodigal son as revealed to us in Luke chapter 15. The son requested his inheritance and then squandered it on riotous living. He eventually ended up with no possessions and had nothing to eat. He would have even eaten the husks that were fed to the swine, but no man would give them to him. Then he made a good decision. He decided to change locations and go back to his father's house.

When he worked his own plan, he was in the filthy hog pen full of lack and considered a nobody without influence on others. The Bible tells us that when he moved to the place of blessing, his father's house, he lived in a nice place, full of abundance, and was a somebody with opportunity to help and influence others for good.

Even Jesus had to change locations to receive the full protection of his Father. After the birth of Jesus, Joseph, the earthly father of Jesus, received several warnings from God in a dream to change locations to get under the protection of God.

"And being warned of God in a dream that they should not return to Herod, they departed into their own country another way. And when they were departed, the angel of the Lord appeareth to Joseph in a dream, saying, arise, and take the young child and his mother, and flee into Egypt, and be thou there until I bring thee word: for Herod will seek the young child to destroy him. When he arose, he took the young child and his mother by night, and departed into Egypt. And was there until the death of Herod: that it might be fulfilled which was spoken of the Lord by the prophet, saying, Out of Egypt have I called my son. Then Herod, when he saw that he was mocked of the wise men, was exceeding wroth, and sent forth, and slew all the children that were in Bethlehem, and in all the coasts thereof, from two years old and under, according to the time which he had diligently inquired of the wise men. Then was fulfilled that which was spoken by Jeremy the prophet, saying, In Rama was there a voice heard, lamentation, and weeping, and great mourning, Rachel weeping for her children, and would not be comforted, because they are not" (Matt. 2:12–18).

Even after Herod died, God continued to guide Joseph to locations of protection and blessing, even in the midst of a dangerous world.

"But when Herod was dead, behold, an angel of the Lord appeareth in a dream to Joseph in Egypt, Saying, Arise, and take the young child and his mother, and go to the land of Israel: for they are dead which sought the young child's life. And he arose, and took the young child and his mother, and came to the land of Israel. But when he heard that Aechelaus did reign in Judaea in the room of his father Herod, he was afraid to go thither: not withstanding, being warned of God in a dream, he turned aside into the parts of Galilee: And he came and dwelt in a city called Nazareth: that it might be fulfilled which was spoken by the prophets, He shall be called a Nazarene" (Matt. 2:19–23).

God has great plans for us. When his plans are followed, great things happen.

"And there are also many other things which Jesus did, the which, if they should be written every one, I suppose that even the world itself could not contain the books that should be written. Amen" (John 21:25).

When we obey, or even disobey, the effects are far reaching—well beyond us and our immediate family. Where would you and I be today if Joseph did not get to the location where the blessing and protection of God was waiting for him and his family?

If we will get to the special place of God, the place of protection and blessing, we can be right in the middle of the world or in hiding in Egypt, but our Enemy that wants to kill, steal and destroy will not be able to find us. We will be hidden under the shadow of God's wing. God has great things in store for your life. Go to the place where God can bless and protect you. Rush to the secret place of the Most High God.

There is a place or location spiritually that God wants us to go. He not only wants us to go there, but he wants us to live there and never leave. Only in this place can we truly experience the fullness of the goodness of God in the land of the living. God not only wants us to experience paradise in heaven, but on earth as well.

"Thy kingdom come. Thy will be done on earth, as it is in heaven" (Matt. 6:10).

God wants things on earth to be as they are in heaven. In heaven, there is no sickness, no poverty, no depression, no disappointments, and no bad relationships. There are only things like love, peace, joy, and fulfillment. God wants that for you while you are still on the earth.

"Beloved, I wish above all things that thou mayest prosper and be in health, even as thy soul prospereth" (3 John v. 2).

God has a wonderful location for you to dwell in by the spirit, and it brings all the things in heaven to the earth. This will not automatically happen. We must cooperate with God and yield to God and his plans. That is not as hard as it sounds, once you are in the secret place of the Most High God. That is where God wants you to be.

Psalm 91:1 tells us that God wants us not just to visit, but also to dwell there. When you go to the secret place found in Psalm 91:1, you will find a God of ever-present help in times of trouble. Always run to God and never run from God, because he only wants to do good to you, even if you don't deserve it. His perfect loves covers a multitude of sins and casts out all fears.

"He that dwelleth in the secret place of the most High shall abide under the shadow of the Almighty" (Ps 91:1).

Chapter 2

The Hiding Place

The secret place is a hiding place where we find the protection of the Lord. We have examined the importance of changing locations by looking at natural examples that represent spiritual changes in location. To what location should we go in the spirit? We should go to the hiding place, the secret place of the Most High under the shadow of the Almighty. We should not only go there, but also dwell there. How do we get there? We move into that place by trusting God. We move out of that place by not trusting God.

"I will say to the Lord, He is my refuge and my fortress: my God, in him will I trust" (Ps. 91:2).

We can trust him because God is not a man that can lie. If we stay in the hiding place, we have the ultimate protection, the protection of God.

"Surely he shall deliver thee from the snare of the fowler, and from the noisome pestilence. He shall cover thee with his feathers, and under his wings shalt thou trust: his truth shall be thy shield and buckler" (Ps 91:3–4).

Let's examine the definition of the words used to describe God's protection over us in the secret place described in Psalm 91 verses 1through 4.

Shelter (verse 1) – Something that offers cover from the weather or protection from danger. Synonyms: haven, sanctuary.

We are covered from all outside dangers and the storms of life when we are under the shelter of God.

Shadow (verse 1) – A part of space from which rays of light are cut off by an interposed opaque body. A reflected image. Synonyms: trace, copy.

When we are in the hiding place, the Devil cannot see us, nor can he see our weaknesses. All he can see is a reflected image or copy of God, and the Devil wants no part of that. That is why the Devil could not find the young child Jesus when his father took him to the right location in the middle of Egypt, which represents the world. He was hidden because he was in the right location. We can be in the middle of the world, doing our jobs, serving God and the Enemy cannot see us to harm us.

Refuge (verse 2) – Shelter or protection from danger or distress. Something to which one has recourse in difficulty. Synonyms: escape, flee.

The hiding place is a place free from distress where we can escape our dangers and difficulties by giving them to our daddy to handle.

Fortress (verse 2) – A place from which one can resist attack, a fortified place. Synonym: stronghold, fort.

It is a place where we are set free from the strongholds of the Enemy and are under the tender, loving, life-giving, healing stronghold of God where we are free from attack.

Feathers (verse 4) – The part of a wing that produces flight. Persons grouped together because they have something in common. A mark of distinction, honor, such as a feather in one's cap. Synonym: to fly, nature.

Under his feathers, we are lifted up in flight above our problems. We are lifted up to God, having something in common with him. Like him, we look down on our problems, and we have the same kind of nature as God. We are above all our problems, free from all hurts.

Wings (verse 4) – A means of flight readily available. Under one's wing: under one's protection: in one's care. A group or faction holding distinct opinion or policies. Synonyms: flying, faction.

Under the wings of God, we are under the care and protection of God who holds a strict policy of no intervention of the Enemy.

Shield (verse 4) – A broad piece of defensive armor carried on the arm. One that protects or defends. A police officer's badge. Synonym: defense.

The shield of God is a complete defense. The shield also represents a threat from God to all demonic forces that might come against us. The Lord uses it to show his badge to the Enemy, so the Enemy knows that to come against us, he must come against the authority of God.

Bulwark (verse 4) – A solid wall-like structure raised for defense: A strong support or projection. Something that holds up or serves as a foundation for something else. Synonyms: rampart, support.

His truth supports us, holds us up, and protects us. It is our foundation. Without the truth of God we will not stand. The secret place is a place where we can find the truth without the distracting noise of this world.

These first four verses of Psalm 91 reveal a great deal about God's character, the way he cares about us, and the freedom he has given us. The words "he who dwelleth" tell us that God lets us choose where we want to live. He doesn't want us to try to live on our own away from his protection, but he has made where we live our choice. That tells us that people in need of protection or who need to be rescued have to first want and accept the help of God and cooperate with those that God is using to bless and help them. If not, even the efforts of anointed people led by God to help will fall short and be unsuccessful.

All of the instruments of protection such as shadow, wings, shield, etc. cover us while we are about the Father's business. When we need separation from the world, we have remedies, such as the fortress. When we are waiting out temporary conditions, we have a shelter, as in under his wings. God desires us to be under his protection because he wants to deliver us from the snare of the fowler and from contagious diseases. The Devil has traps set for us from which God wants to protect us. This won't work if we are doing our own thing with our own ambition. If we seek God's protection because we trust him, then the traps of this world meant for us will be frustrated.

"Thou shalt not be afraid for the terror by night; nor for the arrow that flieth by day; Nor for the pestilence that walketh in darkness; nor for the destruction that wasteth at noonday. A thousand shall fall at thy side, and ten thousand at thy right hand; but it shall not come nigh thee. Only with thine eyes shalt thou behold and see the reward of the wicked. Because thou hast made the LORD, which is my refuge, even the most High, thy habitation; There shall no evil befall thee, neither shall any plague come nigh thy dwelling. For he shall give his angels charge over thee, to keep thee in all thy ways. They shall bear thee up in thy hands, lest thou dash thy foot against a stone. Thou shalt tread upon the lion and the adder: the young lion and the dragon shalt thou trample under feet. Because he hath set his love upon me, therefore will I deliver him: I will set him on high, because he hath known my name. He shall call upon me, and I will answer him: I will be with him in trouble; I will deliver him, and honor him. With long life will I satisfy him, and shew him my salvation" (Ps. 91:5–16).

God has given us great promises in exchange for our abiding in the secret place. If we live there, we are covered by the shadow of God. Yes, the actual shadow of almighty God will cover our life.

Listed below are the promises we receive when we trust God completely and dwell in the secret place:

1. We will not be afraid.

2. No evil shall befall us.

3. No plague shall come near our dwelling.

4. Angels will have charge over us to keep us in all of our ways.

The closer we get to God, the harder it is to hold on to our fears. The longer we stay in the secret place, the more we experience his presence and his goodness. Once we get a taste of his goodness, nothing else will satisfy us.

"O, taste and see that the Lord is good: blessed is the man that trusteth in him" (Ps. 34:8).

Years ago, our family had a cat named Daisy. We raised Daisy from a kitten as she was born in our house. We gave away all the other kittens, but we decided to keep Daisy and make her strictly a house cat. In fact, Daisy never went outside her whole life. When Daisy was about three years old, the door to the attached garage was left open and the overhead garage door was open as well. Daisy approached the threshold, gazed out toward the outside world, and with fear and trembling put one paw on the concrete garage floor. Her paw had barely touched ground before she scurried back into the house, grateful that she suffered no damage and with an apparent resolve never to leave her safe haven again.

That is exactly how I feel whenever I wander out of the shadow of the wing of God. When I realize what I have done, I scurry back into the hiding place of God, the special place of God's love, protection, provision, and blessing.

When we are stationed under the shadow of God's wing, God protects us as a mother hen protects her young. Jesus longs to hold us and laments when we resist his love and his protection.

"O Jerusalem, Jerusalem, which killest the prophets, and stonest them that are sent unto thee; how often would I have gathered thy children together, as a hen doth gather her brood under her wings, and you would not! Behold, your house is left desolate: and verily I say unto you, Ye shall not see, until the time come when ye shall say, Blessed is he that cometh in the name of the Lord" (Luke 13:34–35).

I'm told that a mother hen uses four different calls to her brood. The first is when the hen senses that night is coming. She will call them a certain way, the young chicks will come running and she will gather them under her wing. The second call the mother hen uses is when she sees danger coming, such as a hawk flying above. Once again, the little chicks will come running to get under her wings for protection.

A third special call occurs when the hen finds some good food. She will call out and once again, her chicks come running. The fourth call is when she simply desires to have them close to her. That is the most special one of them all. That call is continually coming from our Lord Jesus to his people. He always wants us with him and has even invited us to dwell there! He calls out to us even now just as he cried out to Jerusalem when he walked the earth.

God says he wants to cover us with his feathers and place us under his wings. Why? He sees that darkness is coming. He sees there is danger overhead. He has special provision for us, and above all, he just desires for us to be with him and close to him. We will be safe and secure under his wings.

He is always calling because there is always darkness in the world. There is always danger in the world. He always wants to give us abundance and special food, and he always desires our intimate fellowship. In other words, he just wants to love us, do good to us, and satisfy our mouths with good things.

God is not someone to run from but someone to run to. There is no one else who can satisfy you like God. The closer we get to God, the more we understand this. The Scriptures instruct us to boldly approach God.
"Let us therefore come boldly unto his throne of grace, that we may obtain mercy, and find grace to help in time of need" (Heb. 4:16).

"For in the time of trouble he shall hide me in his pavilion: in the secret of his tabernacle shall he hide me; he shall set me upon a rock" (Ps. 27:5).

The deeper the relationship Moses developed with God, the bolder he became in approaching God. When God first called to him, Moses was afraid even to look toward God. The closer he got to God and the longer he stayed in close fellowship with God, the more he wanted to stay in God's presence. As Moses saw God work signs, miracles and wonders for the people, he trusted God more and more and wanted to get closer and closer to God. Finally, Moses boldly asked God to show him his glory.

"And he said, I beseech thee, shew me thy glory. And he said, I will make all my goodness pass before thee, and I will proclaim the name of the LORD before thee; and will be gracious to whom I will be gracious, and will shew mercy on whom I will shew mercy. And he said, Thou canst not see my face: for there shall no man see, and live. And the LORD said, Behold, there is a place by me, and thou shalt stand upon a rock: And it shall come to pass, while my glory passeth by, that I will put thee in a clift of the rock, and will cover thee with my hand while I pass by: And I will take away mine hand, and thou shalt see my back parts: but my face shall not be seen" (Ex. 33:18–23).

God said his goodness would pass before Moses. God saw his goodness and his glory as one and the same. It is God's goodness that gives him his glory. His goodness toward us is beyond what our minds can hold. God said to Moses and is saying to you and me: there is a place where we can see God's glory and his goodness. That place is available in the rock, the Rock of Ages, the Lord Jesus Christ.

Jesus has made a way for us to dwell in the presence of God and experience all his goodness and glory. God did not fuss at Moses for presuming he could see God's glory. No, he showed him all of himself that Moses could receive without harm. The closer we get to God, the more we trust and obey, the more of God's goodness and glory we can see and experience, for we have a new and better covenant than Moses had.

To get in the secret place we must trust God. It takes trust to stay there so we can dwell there. Trust only comes from the knowledge of the goodness of God. The most important factor in walking in all the benefits of Psalm 91 is knowledge of the goodness of God.

Chapter 3

God's Plan for Man

People want to know what God is really like, but most folks think it is impossible to know for sure. I suppose that while we are still on this earth we can never know everything there is to know about God. Most people feel that it's hard to know what God is like because he is far away up in heaven and we are down here on the earth. The Scriptures however, reveal a great deal to us about the nature and character of God. Not only do most people today want to know what God is like, but even the disciples who walked with Jesus wanted to know more about our Father in heaven. One day Philip inquired of Jesus that he might show him what the father is like.

"Philip saith unto him, Lord, shew us the Father, and it sufficeth us. Jesus saith unto him, Have I been so long time with you, and yet hast thou not known me, Philip? he that hath seen me has seen the Father; and how sayest thou then, Shew us the Father? Believest thou not that I am in the Father, and the Father in me? the words that I speak unto you I speak not of myself: but the Father that dwelleth in me, he doeth the works (John 14:8–10).

Jesus said that if you have seen him, then you have seen the Father. Jesus only said what the Father told him to say and he only did what the Father told him to do. That's because he came not to do his own will but the will of the Father.

"I can of my own self do nothing: as I hear, I judge: and my judgment is just; because I seek not my own will, but the will of the Father which hath sent me" (John 5:30).

Jesus was a perfect reflection of the Father. He came in the form of a man so that humanity could see who God really is. If we want to know what God is like, all we have to do is read about how Jesus dealt with people in the books of Matthew, Mark, Luke, and John. How did Jesus deal with people? The Bible tells us that he went about teaching, preaching and healing. In fact, the life of Jesus is summarized in this Scripture:

"How God anointed Jesus of Nazareth with the Holy Ghost and with power: who went about doing good, and healing all that were oppressed of the devil; for God was with him" (Acts 10:38).

The way Jesus dealt with people in the books of Matthew, Mark, Luke and John is the same way he deals with people today, because "God is no respecter of persons" (Acts 10:34b) and "Jesus Christ the same yesterday, and today and forever" (Heb.13:8). How did Jesus deal with people? He did good and healed them by operating in the anointing. How did the anointing manifest? Let's read some Scriptures to find out.

"And Jesus departed from thence, and came nigh unto the Sea of Galilee; and went up into a mountain, and sat down there. And great multitudes came unto him, having with them those that were lame, blind, dumb, and many others, and cast them down at Jesus' feet; and he healed them: in so much that the multitude wondered, when they saw the dumb to speak, the maimed to be whole, the lame to walk, and the blind to see: and they glorified the God of Israel" (Matt. 15:29–31).

"But he was wounded for our transgressions, he was bruised for our iniquities: the chastisement of our peace was upon him: and with his stripes we are healed" (Isa. 53:5).
Jesus never turned away anyone who came to him in faith. He always blessed; he always healed. He healed the good people and he healed the bad people. Anyone that showed him some faith got some grace. He desired that everyone come into the family of God so that they could eat at the king's table continually.

That is what God is like. We need knowledge of that. We need to dwell upon his goodness that grace and peace be multiplied to us, that we will have everything we need for life and godliness. So, I'm happy to tell you about the goodness of God in the land of the living.

We need that good reinforcement because we have all kinds of wrong messages that come to us in this life from people that just misunderstand and don't know the goodness of God. Most of them have good motives, but they are just ignorant. I would not have you ignorant brethren but that you would come to know the goodness of God. This lack of knowledge of the goodness of God destroys people.

"My people are destroyed for the lack of knowledge" (Hos. 4:6a).

The lack of knowledge that enables the Enemy to destroy the most is the lack of knowledge of the goodness of God. If you don't know God is good, you won't trust God. If you are not trusting God, then you are afraid. When you are in fear, it creates an open door for the Enemy, and what he does is kill, steal, and destroy. Fear brings destruction "but through knowledge shall the just be delivered" (Prov. 11:9).

God has a wonderful plan for each and every one of us. Many people wonder what God thinks of them, especially when they have done wrong. But God's thoughts for us never change because he never changes.

"For I know the thoughts that I think toward you, saith the LORD, thoughts of peace, and not of evil, to give you an expected end" (Jer. 29:11).

God is for you and not against you! God is with us and God is for us; and "if God be for us, who can be against us?" (Rom. 8:31).

Not only does God have a wonderful plan to bless us; the Devil has an evil plan to destroy us. Satan's strategy and plan of attack have not changed since the Garden of Eden, and we should not be ignorant of his devices. His plan is still the same, and that plan is to get you to doubt the goodness of God. God's desire is to bless you, and it has always been his desire to bless you.

"For I am the LORD, I change not (Mal. 3:6a).

"Jesus Christ the same yesterday, and to day, and for ever" (Heb. 13:8).

If we want to know what God's desire is for us today, we can see what it was from the very beginning, because he never changes. Let's examine the Devil's tactics and God's plan from the very beginning.

Just imagine how God felt when man, immediately after receiving life, looked back into the face of God. I imagine that it would be very similar to the way a mother feels when she first holds her newborn and that baby looks back into his mother's eyes. Out of the depth of their mutual being comes a tremendous love and intimacy. God's love and desire for intimacy with us is even greater than a mother's with her child.

"Can a woman forget her suckling child, that she should not have compassion on the son of her womb? yea, they may forget, yet will I not forget thee" (Isa. 49:15).

The first thing God did after creating man was to place him in paradise. It was paradise because there were no worries, just like in heaven. God still wants it today on earth as it is in heaven, so he invites us to cast all of our cares on him. God wanted us in paradise, so he placed man in a beautiful garden.

"And the LORD God formed man out of the dust of the ground, and breathed into his nostrils the breath of life; and man became a living soul. And the LORD God planted a garden eastward in Eden; and there he put the man whom he had formed" (Gen. 2:7–8).

So immediately after giving life to man, God placed man in a beautiful garden in which there was the same love and harmony in which God had formed and created man. In the Garden of Eden there was no discord, no sin, no sickness, no disharmony—nothing that would bring unrest. There was only peace, joy, communication, and fellowship between God and man. From the start, God extended his goodness toward man on earth. God showed his love and trust placing Adam in the garden and giving him dominion over everything in the garden, even the fruit of the trees, except one. In order for man to be man, he had to be able to say yes or no. Man had to be able to respond to and react to God by his own choices.

God doesn't want robots, and neither do you with your children. I remember when my two children were young. When I came home from work, no matter what they were doing, they would run to greet me, throw their arms around my neck, and tell me that they love me. That brought great joy to me. It was and still is more precious than anything that money can buy.

What if I had come home but instead of running to greet me, my children just sat in place watching television. If I had to threaten them to get them to say they love me, honor me, and obey my words and my voice, it just wouldn't be the same. I want a real love because they choose to love me. God wants the same thing from us, his children.

The Devil, in the form of a serpent, knew that man had to make a choice to follow God or to be a god unto himself. Satan then planted the seed of doubt – to doubt the goodness of God in the mind of man.

"Now the serpent was more subtil than any beast of the field which the LORD God had made. And he said unto the woman, Yea, hath God said, Ye shall not eat of every tree of the garden? And the woman said unto the serpent, We may eat of the fruit of the trees of the garden: But of the fruit of the tree which is in the midst of the garden, God hath said, Ye shall not eat of it, neither shall ye touch it, lest ye die. And the serpent said unto the woman, Ye shall not surely die: For God doth know that in the day ye eat thereof, then your eyes shall be opened, and ye shall be as gods, knowing good and evil. And when the woman saw that the tree was good for food, and that it was pleasant to the eyes, and a tree to be desired to make one wise, she took of the fruit thereof, and did eat, and gave also unto her husband with her; and he did it. And the eyes of them both were opened, and they knew that they were naked; and they sewed fig leaves together, and made themselves aprons" (Gen. 3:1–7).

God has a good plan for your life and the Devil has an evil plan for your life. It is up to you to choose. Jesus shed his blood and died for whosoever will enter in to a blood covenant with him and become a joint equal heir with him as a child of the king. Each one of us, like Mephibosheth, must accept or reject the blood covenant.

The Devil's plan for your life is diagramed below.

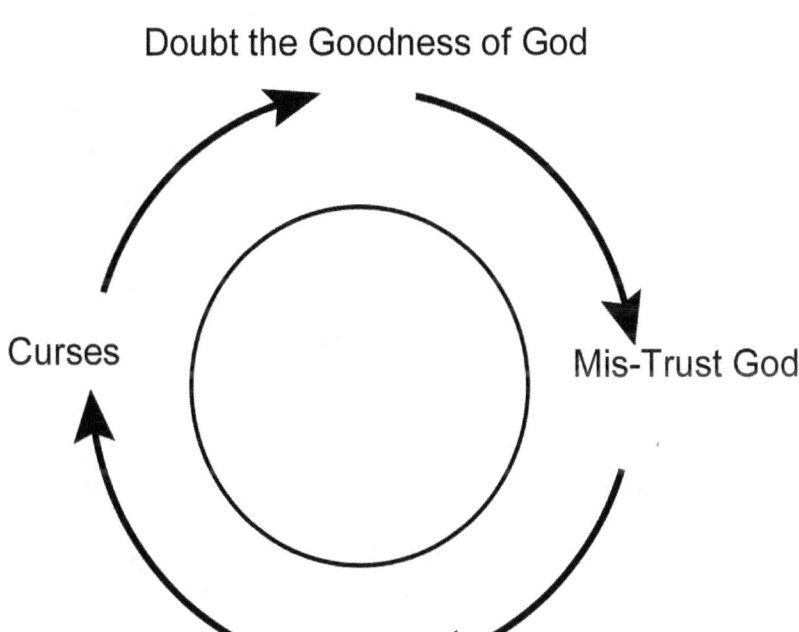

The Enemy's first priority is to get you to doubt the goodness of God. He will resort to anything to accomplish this. He will call God a liar.

"Ye shall not surely die" (Gen. 3:4b).

He will twist the truth to make you believe that God is holding back something good from you.
"For God doth know that in the day ye eat thereof, then your eyes shall be opened, and ye shall be as gods, knowing good and evil" (Gen. 3:5).

God has not held back any good thing from us. God is not a stingy God but a loving, giving, and generous God as revealed in the following Scriptures:

"For the LORD God is a sun and a shield: the LORD will give peace and glory: no good thing will he withhold from them that walk uprightly. O LORD of hosts, blessed is the man that trusteth in thee" (Ps. 84: 11–12).

"The Spirit beareth witness with our spirit that we are the children of God: and if children, then heirs; heirs of God, joint heirs with Christ" (Rom. 8:16–17a).

"Fear not little flock; for it is your Father's good pleasure to give you the kingdom" (Luke 12:32).

"According as his divine power hath given unto us all things that pertain unto life and godliness, through the knowledge of him that hath called us to glory and virtue: Whereby are given unto us exceeding great and precious promises: that by these ye might be partakers of the divine nature, having escaped the corruption that is in the world through lust" (2 Pet. 1: 3–4).

God doesn't have anything bad to give us. He just has good things for us. If it is not from God, we should not want it or take it, but if it is from God, we know it must be good.

"Every good gift and every perfect gift is from above, and cometh down from the Father of lights, with whom is no variableness, neither shadow of turning" (James 1:17).

God is always good and he will not vary from that goodness. He will not turn from his goodness with even a shadow of a turn. Praise the Lord! The Devil, who Jesus said was the father of all lies, will lie to us so that we will doubt the goodness of God. There is no truth in the Devil, for God is always good. If we listen and receive the lies of our Enemy, we will mistrust God and go after the good things of this world apart from God. This is foolish because every good and perfect gift comes from God and God alone.

This is what most of the people of this world do. They don't trust God for good things, so they do whatever they think they must to get them, even if it means loss of integrity or violation of kingdom laws. Disobedience naturally flows from mistrust of God. There are always bad consequences when we sin against God, because we always reap what we sow.

"The wages of sin is death; but the gift of God is eternal life through Jesus Christ our Lord" (Rom. 6:23).

"But it shall come to pass, if thou wilt not hearken unto the voice of the LORD thy God, to observe to do all his commandments and his statutes which I command thee this day; that all these curses shall come upon thee, and overtake thee (Deut. 28:15).

The Devil will always show up to falsely accuse God as we face the consequences resulting from our own decision to disobey God. The Devil is not only the accuser of the brethren, but he also is the accuser of God. It was our mistrust of a faithful and true God that led to our trouble. The Enemy will point the finger at God and say, "Look what God has done to you." Yet, if we would have trusted God and obeyed, we could have been blessed.

If we believe the Devil's accusations against God then even more we will doubt the goodness of God. Then we will mistrust God more. Then we will disobey God more. Then more curses will manifest in our lives, and we will even more doubt the goodness of God. We will be trapped in a downward spiral, and things will get worse and worse. This is the Devil's plan for your life.

Satan's plan is for you to live your life in need, broken and in bondage to drugs, alcohol, and other destructive, addictive behaviors, have all your relationships ruined, and then die young from sickness with nobody to care if you live or die.

God's plan for you is completely the opposite. He wants to satisfy you with a long life full of meaning, full of abundance and full of health and strength. He desires that your life would count for something leaving a wonderful legacy to pass on to the many who love you. His perfect will for you is to live a long, full, healthy life that fulfills a wonderful kingdom destiny. Then when it is your time to go, you lay your head down while in perfect health and peacefully go to be with the Lord, leaving a good inheritance even to your children's children.

The plan of God for your life is diagramed below.

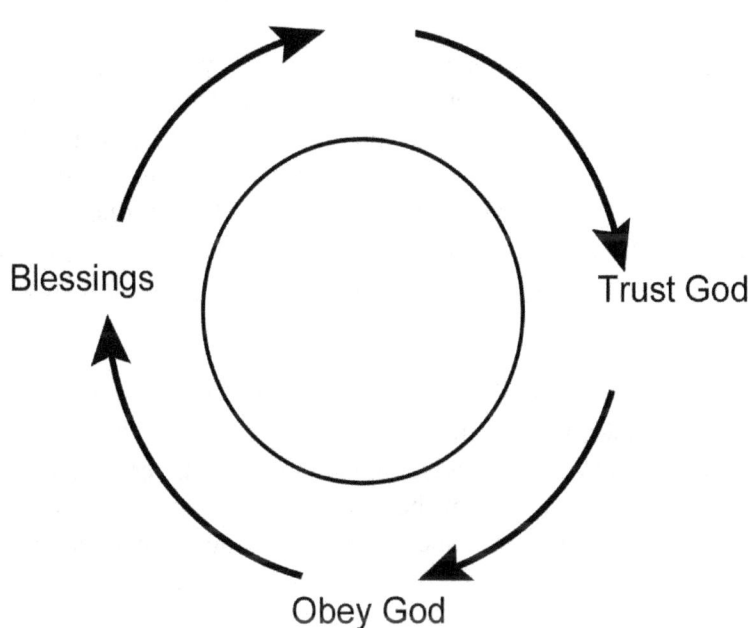

If you are convinced that God is good and always for you and never against you, then you are well on your way to fulfilling your kingdom destiny. If you have the knowledge that God is not withholding something good from you, then you can trust God. That trust gives you the liberty to obey God because you know it is for your good always. That obedience will bring the blessings of God as God has placed that spiritual law into the earth.

"And it shall come to pass, if thou shalt hearken diligently unto the voice of the LORD thy God, to observe and to do all of his commandments which I command thee this day, that the LORD thy God will set thee on high above all nations of the earth: And all these blessings shall come on thee, and overtake thee, if thou shalt hearken unto the voice of the LORD thy God" (Deut. 28:1–2).

When you see the blessings of God in your life, you will come to understand to an even greater degree how good God is. The more you increase in the knowledge of the goodness of God, the more you will trust him, the more you will obey him, the more you will be blessed and the more you'll be convinced of his goodness. Then things just keep getting better and better. This is the perfect plan of God for your life. The Devil's plan has a cycle of death but God's plan has a cycle of life.

"For this cause we also, since the day we heard it, do not cease to pray for you, and to desire that ye might be filled with the knowledge of his will in all wisdom and spiritual understanding: That ye might walk worthy of the lord unto all pleasing, being fruitful in every good work, and increasing in the knowledge of God" (Col. 1:9–10).

As we are filled with the knowledge of God's will to do good to us and to heal us of all the oppression of the Devil, then we will walk worthy of the Lord in the path that he has chosen. We won't go to the right or to the left, because we trust God. That trust puts us under the shadow of his wing. We will please the Lord and produce fruit in every good work, and then increase more in the knowledge of the goodness, faithfulness, and character of God. This verse is a word picture of the above diagram of God's will for our lives.

God is always giving us opportunities to get into a position or place in which he can bless us. We just have to listen to him, yield to him, trust him, and obey him. Let me remind you how God thinks about you.

"For I know the thoughts that I think towards you, saith the LORD, thoughts of peace, and not of evil, to give you an expected end" (Jer. 29:11).

God's thoughts toward us are always good. How often does God think those good thoughts about us? The Scriptures give us the answer.

"How precious also are thy thoughts unto me, O God! how great is the sum of them! If I should count them, they are more in number than the sand: when I awake, I am still with thee" (Ps. 139:17–18).

"Many, O LORD my God, are thy wonderful works which thou hast done, and thy thoughts which are to us-ward: they cannot be reckoned up in order unto thee: if I would declare and speak of them, they are more than can be numbered" (Ps. 40:5).

The good thoughts of peace, hope, and love from God toward us are more than can be numbered. In other words, God is always—24 hours a day and 7 days a week—thinking something good about you. When you wake up in the morning, God is thinking something good about you. During the day, all day long, God is thinking something good about you. When you are at home or wherever you might be in the evening, God is thinking something good about you. As you are sleeping, God is looking at you through the eyes of the greatest love ever known and thinking good thoughts about you. When you awake, he is still with you.

When my children were infants, my wife and I would look over our children while they were sleeping. We would look at them with such love, and we were really in awe of what God had done through the gift of life and how precious our children were to us. Today, as they are adults, we still feel the same way about them. I can remember looking at them while they lay sleeping in their cribs and thinking how innocent and pure they were. That is how God looks at us. His eyes are always upon us because he loves us so much. When the blood of Jesus is applied to our lives, God sees us as pure and innocent even into our adulthood. It's not because of our performance but because the blood of Jesus makes us as innocent as Jesus, the son of God.

God is always for us and never against his children. Think about all the Little League baseball games you have attended. When his child was at bat, have you ever heard a father exhort the pitcher by shouting, "Strike him out!" My wife, Sandy, and I have attended twenty-three consecutive pre-school graduations at our church's Possibility School. The children have done various things to perform and sing before their parents and other loved ones. Of course, they did not do everything perfectly and, in fact, it was normal for them to make lots of mistakes. Even though that was true, as I looked at the faces of each parent over a twenty-three year period, I never saw anything but a big smile reflecting the love and pride that they had for their children. If earthly parents feel that way, how much more does our heavenly Father love us and feel proud of us, even though we make mistakes?

"For both he that sanctifieth and they who are sanctified are all of one: for which cause he is not ashamed to call them brethren" (Heb. 2:11).

"If ye then, being evil, know how to give good gifts unto your children, how much more shall your Father which is in heaven give good things to them that ask him?" (Matt. 7:11).

God has a wonderful plan for your life, and the Devil has an evil plan for your life. God has given you a free will so you make the choice, not God. God has done everything he can to help you make the right choice, but he can't make it for you. Please listen to God and make the right choice.

"I call heaven and earth to record this day against you, that I have set before you life and death, blessing and curses: therefore choose life, that both thou and thy seed may live: That thou mayest love the Lord thy God, and that thou mayest obey his voice, and that thou mayest cleave unto him: for he is thy life, and length of thy days: that thou mayest dwell in the land which the LORD sware unto thy fathers, to Abraham, to Isaac, and to Jacob, to give them" (Deut. 30:19–20).

Chapter 4

Que Sera, Sera
Whatever Will Be, Will Be

Que Sera, Sera (Whatever Will Be Will Be) by Jay Livingston and Ray Evans was a popular song in the 1950s sung by Doris Day and featured in the 1956 Alfred Hitchcock movie starring James Stewart entitled *The Man Who Knew Too Much.* The lyrics of that song mimic some religious thinking resulting from the deception of the Devil. Such thinking has caused many of God's people to doubt the goodness of God. If our thinking lines up with the philosophy of these lyrics, then we would be a person who knows too little. (I do recommend the movie if you ever get a chance to see it.)

Que será, será is an idiom in the Spanish language. In English, it translates to whatever will be, will be. This implies that what we do or say today makes no difference in our future and that we have absolutely no control over the outcome of our lives.

The song's lyrics tell us that we can't know anything about our future. These lyrics do not reflect the truth of the spiritual laws that God has established on this earth. In fact, your life right now is based on the thoughts you have had and the words that have come out of your mouth in the past. You are shaping your future based on what you say today, and what you say today is based on what you think in your heart. We will go over this concept in more detail in the chapter about changing our thinking. Many people today, and even most preachers, think that everything that happens on the earth is caused by God and that he approves everything before it

can happen. If that's true, then God has not truly given us a free will.
We were given dominion over the things of this world. God established man's dominion from the very moment he created us.

"And God said, Let us make man in our image, after our likeness: and let them have dominion over the fish of the sea, and over the fowl of the air, and over the cattle, and over all the earth, and over every creeping thing that creepeth upon the earth. So God created man in his own image, in the image of God created he him; male and female created he them. And God blessed them, and God said unto them, Be fruitful, and multiply, and replenish the earth, and subdue it: and have dominion over the fish of the sea, and over the fowl of the air, and over every living thing that moveth upon the earth" (Gen. 1: 26–28).

Notice how God said, "let <u>us</u> make man" but "let <u>them</u> have dominion." God is not to take dominion over the affairs of the earth because he gave that task to you and me.

"The heaven, even the heavens, are the LORD's: but the earth hath he given to the children of men" (Ps. 115:16).

We are to use our free will to freely live under God's authority as ambassadors to earth and do the will of the Father just as Jesus did. We take dominion because God has given us the authority to do it. We are made in the likeness of God to function like God on this earth.

"Now then we are ambassadors for Christ, as though God did beseech you by us: we pray you in Christ's stead, be ye reconciled to God" (2 Cor. 5: 20).

An ambassador is supposed to do the will of the country or kingdom he represents. If I am a good ambassador, I don't do what I think is best, but I do the will of and represent the one who sent me. Jesus was the perfect example.

Man lost his dominion through sin, but Jesus came and restored back to us everything that Adam had lost.

"Therefore as by the offence of the judgement came upon all men to condemnation: even so by the righteousness of one free gift upon all men unto justification of life. For as by one man's disobedience many were made sinners, so by the obedience of one shall many be made righteous" (Rom. 5: 18–19).

To change things on the earth, Jesus, the second and last Adam, had to come to earth as a man, because God gave dominion in the earth to man, not to himself. Jesus, as a sinless man, has put us back in the same place of dominion that Adam and Eve had before sin entered the earth. The difference for us now is that we have to deal with the effects of sin, as it is still prevalent on the earth. This means that even more we must take dominion over the systems of this world and give the system of the Kingdom of God a place of dominance.

Man is a spiritual being like our God. Yet man was also meant to rule in the physical realm. Therefore, God gave physical bodies to mankind. Jesus came as God in the physical body of a man to set things in order on the earth. To loose his power on the earth, God always uses a man, woman, boy, or girl, in a human body, because God has said, "let them have dominion." God does not stray from what he declares.

"God is not a man, that he should lie; neither the son of a man, that he should repent: hath he said, and shall he not do it? or hath he spoken, and shall he not make it good?" (Num. 23:19).

God is legally bound to work through willing people, and he is not a lawless one like Satan. We are the ones that have to cooperate with God to make good things on earth as they are in heaven. Without God, we cannot; but without us, God will not. Many people believe that everything that happens is God's will. Every murder, sickness, rape, and child molestation is God's will? That is so far from the truth. If God controls everything, then we shouldn't prosecute a child molester, because, after all, God was in control of that situation. We shouldn't pray to be healed, because God is in control. There is no sickness in God and he can't give you what he doesn't have.

Not everything that happens in this earth is God's will. God's will is as it is in heaven. He wants to use you and me to bring his will on earth as it is in heaven. The Bible says that God does not want anyone to perish, yet we know that people die and go to hell every day. Therefore, his will is not always done on earth.

"The Lord is not slack concerning his promise, as some men count slackness; but is longsuffering to us-ward, not willing that any should perish, but that all should come to repentance" (2 Pet. 3:9).

If we want to see God's will of blessing in people's lives because they repent, simply tell them of the goodness of God. Telling them that they have messed up won't accomplish much because people already know that. The thing that produces the most fruit is to tell them of the goodness of God.

"Or depiseth thou the riches of his goodness and forbearance and longsuffering: not knowing that the goodness of God leadeth thee to repentence?" (Rom. 2:4).

God has given us a free will and he lets us use it. God was not taken by surprise when Adam was about to take a bite of the fruit from the tree of the knowledge of good and evil. God was not caught napping. God knew the horrible and long-lasting devastation to mankind that would result from this sin. Yet God allowed Adam to eat because he had given Adam a free will. God did not reach down and knock the fruit out of Adam's hand. God is in control of your life only if you let him be in control.

What about tribulations that happen to good people who are yielded to God? We will cover this in a later chapter, but know that those who trust in the Lord will not be ashamed. If we will trust God, he will turn even tribulations to our good.

"For we know all things work together for good to them that love God, to them that are called according to his purpose" (Rom. 8:28).

Each one of us makes the choice to put God in control, because we trust him, or to control our own life. God lets us choose.

"And if it seems evil unto you to serve the LORD, choose you this day whom you will serve; whether the gods which your fathers served that were on the other side of the flood, or the gods of the Amorites, in whose land ye dwell: but as for me and my house, we will serve the LORD" (Josh. 24:15).

God works with faithful men and women to bring about change on this earth. The people of God have dominion, and it's up to us to make life on earth as it is in heaven. It's time to quit blaming government and the ungodly for the problems in our nation. God says it's up to his people to bring healing and peace.

"If my people, which are called by my name, shall humble themselves, and pray, and seek my face, and turn from there wicked ways; then will I hear from heaven, and will forgive their sin, and will heal their land" (2 Chron. 7:14).

God has given man authority on the earth. He will not intervene on earth without the cooperation of a human clothed in flesh.

"Thus saith the LORD, the Holy One of Israel, and his Maker, Ask me of things to come concerning my sons, and concerning the works of my hands command ye me" (Isa 45:11).

Do we command God? No, but when we command a thing in obedience to him, it is God who performs it. We do not beg God to do things, instead we command them to be done as God commanded us to do. Since we can't do it alone, and God won't do it without us, we are, in effect, commanding the works of his hands.

"For verily I say unto you, That whosoever shall say unto this mountain, Be thou removed, and be thou cast into the sea; and shall not doubt in his heart, but shall believe that those things which he saith shall come to pass; he shall have whatsoever he saith" (Mark 11:23).

Even though God has chosen to work with man and has given man dominion over this earth, we can be assured that God's overall plan and the things he has spoken will come to pass on the earth. God will always find someone who will yield to him. After all, it only takes one man for God to move. If we move, God will be with us.

When we neglect to pray or to obey God, we are forfeiting the manifested realization of our dominion and authority.

"Yet ye have not, because ye ask not" (James 4:2b).

You see, we choose the harvest that we receive.

"Be not deceived; God is not mocked: for whatsoever a man soweth, that shall he also reap" (Gal. 6:7).

When we walk our own way, we allow God's purposes on the earth to be hindered or delayed. It is awesome to think that the God of the universe trusts you and me to get his work done.

"I will give unto thee the keys of the kingdom of heaven: and whatsoever thou shalt bind on earth shall be bound in heaven: and whatsoever thou shalt loose on earth shalt be loosed in heaven" (Matt. 16:19).

God's people are equipped to walk and talk like God on the earth as we "calleth those things that be not as though they were" (Rom. 4:17b).

Since we are made in the image of God, we have creative power when we believe in our hearts and speak with our mouths. Since dominion was given to man, God uses obedient people to speak on the earth.

"Surely the LORD God will do nothing, but he revealeth his secret unto his servants the prophets" (Amos 3:7).

The Devil needs people to accomplish his will on the earth as well. He cannot accomplish anything without man, because Jesus won the victory for us and took back the authority for man.

"And you, being dead in your sins and the uncircumcision of your flesh, hath he quickened together with him, having forgiven you all trespasses; Blotting out the handwriting of ordinances that was against us, which was contrary to us, and took it out of the way, nailing it to his cross; And having spoiled principalities and powers, he made a shew of them openly, triumphing over them in it" (Col. 2:13–15).

The Devil oppresses people made in the image of God, so they speak into existence what he wants so he can kill, steal, and destroy. God blesses people made in the image of God so they can speak into existence what *he* wants so he can bring life, gifts, and restoration.

The battleground is the mind. That's why God has said that we should keep our minds "stayed upon the Lord" so that we can have perfect peace. We should think and meditate on the goodness of God.

"Finally, brethren, whatsoever things are true, whatsoever things are honest, whatsoever things are just, whatsoever things are pure, whatsoever things are lovely, whatsoever things are of good report; if there be any virtue, and if there be any praise, think on these things" (Phil 4:8).

Our minds should be renewed on the Word of God if we want the blessings of God. What we think and therefore do has a great impact on our life. God has said to ask him of things to come. *Que será, será* has no place in the kingdom of God. It is a nice song in a nice movie, but what will be is what we say it will be.

Chapter 5

God Has Not Forgotten You

It is easy to believe that God is good to other people whom we admire, such as Billy Graham. The Devil may try to convince you that God may want to bless others but not you. The Devil is a liar and the father of all lies. Sometimes we feel that God is a million miles away. Even people of faith feel that way sometimes. When we go through troubles or sickness or broken relationships, we can feel that God is quite distant from us, even though he has always come through for us. We feel that we can't touch the throne room of God. Yet God has invited us to come boldly into his throne room even when we have messed up.

Various people and salesmen want to come to my office to talk to me. For the most part, I require that they make an appointment. My children, however, can just walk into my office unannounced, and I will always make time for them. If an earthly father will do that for his children, how much more freely will our heavenly Father receive us with joy? We are always welcome in God's throne room, even though sometimes we don't feel we are welcome. God welcomes us based on how he thinks, not on how we think.

The pain you have, God feels it. He is aware of your pain. When you are lonely, or when you have are hurting, God feels what you feel.

"For we have not an high priest which cannot be touched with the feeling of our infirmities; but was in all points tempted like as we are, yet without sin" (Heb. 4:15).

There are times when people disappoint you and let you down, even after you do good things for them. God knows all about that. He is aware of every need you have. Yet sometimes we think God has forgotten us. We have a big problem and wonder if perhaps God has forgotten us. We think that we are down here on the earth trying to do the best we can, and God is far away from us up in heaven. The truth is that God is very near to you.

"A man that hath friends must shew himself friendly: and there is a friend that sticketh closer than a brother" (Prov.18:24).

"And hath raised us up together, and made us sit together in heavenly places in Christ Jesus" (Eph. 2:6).

I want you to know that God remembers you. It is his desire to bless you. It has always been his desire to bless you. God has not forgotten you!

"For God is not unrighteous to forget your work and labour of love, which ye have shewed toward his name, in that ye have ministered to the saints, and do minister."

God remembers every single thing that you have done for him. He remembers every word of encouragement that you spoke to someone who needed it. He remembers every phone call to someone in the hospital. He remembers every prayer you prayed in faith and every time you stood in the gap for someone else. He remembers every time you obeyed his spirit and gave an offering as he directed. He remembers every kind word that you spoke and even each time you smiled at someone. He remembers every time you told someone about Jesus. He especially remembers each time you gave a cookie or poured fruit punch in children's church. God has not forgotten you.

Now let me tell you what God *has* forgotten about you if you know Jesus. God has forgotten your sins and sees you with the righteousness of Jesus. He has removed our sins from us as far as the east is from the west and has thrown them into the sea of forgetfulness to remember them no more.

"As far as the east is from the west, so far hath he removed our transgressions from us" (Ps. 103:12).

"Who is a God like unto thee, that pardoneth iniquity, and passeth by the transgression of the remnant of his heritage? he retaineth not his anger for ever, because he delighteth in mercy. He will turn again, he will have compassion upon us; he will subdue our iniquities; and thou wilt cast all their sins into the depths of the sea" (Mic. 7:18–19).

"I, even I, am he that blotteth out thy transgressions for mine sake, and will not remember thy sins" (Isa. 43:25).

"For I will be merciful to their unrighteousness, and their sins and their iniquities will I remember no more" (Heb. 8:12).

We lament to God about how we did this wrong and messed that up, and his reply is that he doesn't remember any of our sins. You see, the blood of Jesus is not like the blood of a bull or a goat. It doesn't temporarily cover our sins. No, the blood of Jesus *removes* our sins, for Jesus was the once-and-for-all perfect sacrifice.

God is saying to you right now that he doesn't remember your sin, but he does remember the time you stood for him when you boldly spoke the word of God. He remembers when you were intimidated and afraid, but you stood for God anyway because you love him. He remembers your faithfulness. That is how God looks at you. He sees you with great favor, and the favor of God goes a long way. You are not on your own. Let God help you.

"For they got not the land in possession by their own sword, neither did their own arm save them: but thy right hand, and thine arm, and the light of thy countenance, because thou hadst a favour unto them" (Ps. 44:3).

"For thou, LORD, wilt bless the righteous; with favour wilt thou compass him as with a shield" (Ps. 5:12).

Thank God that we don't have to rely on our abilities or skills. We can rely upon the favor of God, and it will do the work. God knows who you are, where you are, how you are, and why you are. He knows every hair on your head. He's with you; he's in you; he's for you. And if God be for you who can be against you?

God remembers you. Don't listen to the Devil who says that God has forgotten you. God has a plan to lift you up and out of your affliction, and at the same time, advance the kingdom. God's favor is on you now.

"Thou shalt arise, and have mercy upon Zion: for the time to favour her, yea, the set time, is come" (Ps. 102:13).

Chapter 6

God Wants You Healed

No one can believe God for healing above his knowledge of God's will for healing. Do you want to know what God's will is? Then let's look at the life of Jesus. Jesus came to show us the Father. What are the works of Father? They are revealed in Acts 10:38 as Jesus showed us the Father.

"How God anointed Jesus of Nazareth with the Holy Ghost and with the power: who went about doing good, and healing all that were oppressed of the devil; for God was with him"(Acts 10:38).

Notice that Jesus didn't do good and bad; he just did good. The whole Word of God is good news. That's why Jesus said to preach good news, not to preach good and bad news. Jesus only said and did what the Father told him to say and do. He only spoke and performed good things. The Word instructs us to do the same because "out of the same mouth proceedeth blessings and curses. My brethren, these things ought not so to be. Doth a fountain send forth at the same place sweet water and bitter?" (James 3:10–11).

Jesus wants us healed and in good health. There exists today some wrong thinking and teaching, which declares that sometimes God makes people sick because of their sin. If that were true, then we would all be sick. "For all have sinned, and come short of the glory of God" (Rom. 3:23). Jesus will not divide his kingdom by both healing and making sick.

In Matthew 12:22–28, Jesus was accused of dividing his kingdom. As usual, Jesus had the answer of good news.

"Then was brought unto him one possessed with a devil, blind and dumb: and he healed him, insomuch the blind and dumb both spake and saw. And all the people were amazed, and said, Is not this the son of David? But the Pharisees heard it, they said this fellow doth not cast out devils, but by Beelzebub the prince of the devils. And Jesus knew their thoughts, and said unto them, Every kingdom divided against itself is brought to desolation; and every city or house divided against itself shall not stand: And if Satan cast out Satan, he is divided against himself; how shall then his kingdom stand? And if I by Beelzebub cast out devils, by whom do your children cast them out? therefore they shall be your judges. But if I cast out devils by the Spirit of God, then the kingdom of God is come unto you" (Matt. 12:22–28).

If Jesus had made even one person sick and then healed, his house would have fallen. Jesus *won't* divide his kingdom by making someone sick. Satan won't divide his kingdom by healing. It's very simple: the Devil brings sickness and Jesus brings healing.

Jesus commissioned the body of Christ to be against sickness and disease and bring healing. We should not accept sickness. If sickness and disease were God's will, then you would have no business asking for healing or going to the doctor. Jesus is the Christ–the anointed one. Let's look again at how the anointing was manifested.

"And Jesus departed from thence, and came nigh unto the Sea of Galilee; and went up into a mountain, and sat down there. And great multitudes came unto him, having with them those that were lame, blind, dumb, and many others, and cast them down at Jesus' feet; and he healed them: insomuch that the multitude wondered, when they saw the dumb to speak, the maimed to be whole, the lame to walk, and the blind to see: and they glorified the God of Israel" (Matt. 15:29-31).

You see, it's the healing that glorifies God; sickness only glorifies the Devil. You can still glorify God when you are sick, but God is never glorified in sickness. Great multitudes came to Jesus and he healed them all. To me, a multitude of people is as many people as the eye can see. A great multitude of people is more than that. Great *multitudes* are even more. Yet Jesus did not turn even one person away but healed them all.

Some people think that God won't heal them because of some bad things they have done. Healing is for whosoever will receive it by faith. It is not based on performance. Don't you think that in great multitudes that there is at least one person whose performance is worse than yours is? Yet, Jesus healed them.

In great multitudes, you will find every kind of person. You'll find rich and poor, young and old, and every ethnic background. In great multitudes, there are educated people and those with no schooling, people from good families and people from bad families. There are those that are married, single, and divorced. There are people with religious training and people who have never even prayed once. There are kind people and mean people. There are people who are sexually pure and those that have performed perversion. There are all kinds of people. Jesus healed them all.

"And Jesus went about all Galilee, teaching in the synagogues. and preaching the gospel of the kingdom, and healing all manner of sickness and all manner of disease among the people. And his fame went throughout all Syria: and they brought unto him all sick people that were taken with divers diseases and torments, and those which were possessed with devils, and those which were lunatick, and those that had the palsy; and he healed them" (Matt. 4:23–24).

Jesus healed all manner of sickness and disease. There is not any kind of sickness and disease that is not subject to the authority of the Lord Jesus Christ. They brought to him all sick people and he healed them. There is not one example in the Bible where Jesus turned away a sick person who came to him to be healed.

He not only healed those who were oppressed in their body but also those who were oppressed in their spirit and in their mind. He healed those who were possessed with devils and those who were lunatic. Remember, Jesus was anointed to go about doing good and healing all who were oppressed of the Devil.

Jesus always healed all that were sick. He *never* said, "I'll heal this one but I won't heal that one."

"When the even was come, they brought unto him many that were possessed with devils: and he cast out the spirits with his word, and healed all that were sick. That it might be fulfilled which was spoken by Esaias the prophet, saying Himself took our infirmities, and bare our sickness" (Matt. 8:16–17).

God's will is for you to be healed. The Bible says: "Beloved, I wish above all things that you prosper and be in health, even as your soul prospers" (3 John v.2).

His will is to come and heal you, if you will ask him.
"And when Jesus was entered into Capernaum, there came unto him a Centurion, beseeching him, And saying, Lord, my servant

lieth at home sick of the palsy, grievously tormented. And Jesus saith unto him, I will come and heal him" (Matt. 8:5–7).

Some people think that God is too busy running the universe or is not concerned with their sickness. They feel that their malady is not important enough for God to respond to their need. The Word of God shows us that Jesus is willing to take the time to heal you, because he is still the same and is not a respecter of persons.

"Now when then the sun was setting, all they that had any sick with divers diseases brought unto him; and he laid his hands on every one of them, and healed them. And devils also came out of many, crying out, and saying, Thou art Christ the Son of God. And he rebuking them suffered them not to speak: for they knew that he was Christ. And when it was day, he departed and went into the desert place: and the people sought him, and came unto him, and stayed him, that he should not depart from them. And he said unto them, I must preach the kingdom of God to other cities also: for therefore am I sent. And he preached in the synagogues of Galilee" (Luke 4:40–44).

Jesus began laying on hands and healing every one of them when the sun was setting. When he had finished touching and healing each one, it was daytime again. Jesus spent twelve hours so that he could touch and heal each and every person. In such a large group as that, surely there were those who felt that their life was not important. Yet to Jesus, they were important enough to take the time to touch and make perfectly whole.

Okay preacher, that was back when Jesus walked on the earth in a body. What about today?

Jesus still has a body today that is walking on the earth (the church). He will deal with you today the same way he dealt with the people then. How? Through an anointing in his body.

"And Jesus went about all the cities and villages, teaching in their synagogues, and preaching the gospel of the kingdom, and healing every sickness and every disease among the people. But when saw the multitudes, he was moved with compassion on them, because they fainted, and were scattered abroad, as sheep having no shepherd. Then saith he unto his disciples, The harvest truly is plenteous, but the labourers are few; Pray ye therefore the Lord of the harvest, that he will send forth labourers into his harvest"(Matt. 9:35–38).

Jesus was moved with compassion when he saw the multitudes with so many needs. Things haven't changed much, have they? We may ride in a car instead of on a donkey, but there are still multitudes of hurting people and few laborers to minister to them.

The answer today is the same as it was then. We have to pray and work. Pray for more laborers but continue to bring in the harvest. Jesus knew that it was a big job for so few. He also knew that the job had to get done. He knew that the few laborers needed big-time power if they were going to reach multitudes of hurting people. So he continued in chapter 10, verse 1.

"And when he had called unto him his twelve disciples, he gave them power against unclean spirits, to cast them out, and to heal all manner of sickness and all manner of disease" (Matt. 10:1).

The body of Christ today has power against unclean spirits and power to heal all manner of sickness and disease. Jesus has commanded us to use that power freely and to reach and heal as many as we can. He instructed his disciples in Matthew 10:8. "Heal the sick, cleanse the lepers, raise the dead, cast out devils: freely ye have received; freely give" (Matt. 10:8).

Okay, preacher, that is how Jesus dealt with the multitudes, but I'm alone and I have no one and I need healing. How will Jesus deal with me?

Let's look and see how Jesus dealt with individuals. Since he is no respecter of persons and is the same today, we know he will deal with you and me in the same manner. Let's see how Jesus dealt with the leper in Matthew 8:1–3.

"When he was come down from mountain, great multitudes followed him. And behold, there came a leper and worshipped him, saying, Lord, if thou wilt, thou canst make me clean. And Jesus put forth his hand, and touched him, saying, I will; be thou clean. And immediately his leprosy was cleansed" (Matt. 8:1–3).

People still ask Jesus this question today. Jesus, are you willing to heal me? His answer is still the same—I am willing. The Devil will try to convince you that God may want to heal others but not you. Because Jesus is no respecter of persons and the same today, his answer to you is this—*I am willing to heal you right where you are, just as you are.*

Let's see how Jesus dealt with the crippled man in John, chapter 5.

"After this there was a feast of the Jews; and Jesus went up to Jerusalem. Now there is at Jerusalem by the sheep market a pool, which is called in the Hebrew tongue Bethesda, having five porches. In these lay a great multitude of impotent folk, of blind, halt, withered, waiting for the moving of the water. For an angel went down at a certain season into the pool, and troubled the water. Whosoever then first after the troubling of the water stepped in was made whole of whatsoever disease he had. And a certain man was there, which had an infirmity thirty and eight years. When Jesus saw him lie, and knew that he had been now a long time in that case, he saith unto him, Wilt thou be made whole? The impotent man answered him, Sir, I have no man, when the water is troubled, to put me into the pool: but while I am coming, another steppeth down before me. Jesus saith unto him, Rise, take up thy bed, and walk. And immediately the man was made whole, and took up his bed, and walked: and on the day was the Sabbath" (John 5:1–9).

Jesus still asks us the same question today: *Do you want to be healed?* If the answer is yes, you will get the same result. Some people really don't want to be healed. They are having too much fun complaining about their situation. They are blaming other people rather than looking to the healer. Jesus is standing right there waiting, but they are too busy blaming others. It doesn't matter who is at fault; Jesus is asking if you want to be healed.

Don't sit by the pool waiting for some sovereign move of God. You might wait thirty-eight years! Sovereign moves of God are unpredictable, but the Bible assures us of the following: Where there is faith, there will always be grace. You can receive the grace of God anytime you release faith to God, and you don't have to wait thirty-eight years.
"Therefore it is of faith, that it might be by grace" (Rom. 4:16a).

Satan wants you to believe that your will is not a factor. His theme song is *Que Sera, Sera, Whatever Will Be, Will Be*. He wants you to think that if you're sick, God must want you to be sick and that if God wants to heal you, he will heal you. After all, he's God and is in charge of everything. This notion is a lie from the Devil. If you choose to sit by the pool, Jesus will let you. You have a free will. Jesus wants to heal you and is asking you, *do you want to be healed?* If so, you call on the name of Jesus and you will not be turned away. Let's see how Jesus dealt with blind Bartimaeus.

"And they came to Jericho: and as he went out of Jericho with his disciples and a great number of people, blind Bartimaeus, the son of Timaeus sat by the highway side begging. And when he heard that if was Jesus of Nazareth, he began to cry out, and say, Jesus, thou son of David, have mercy on me. And many charged him that he should hold his peace: but he cried the more a great deal, thou son of David, have mercy on me. And Jesus stood still. And commanded him to be called. And they call the blind man, saying unto him, be of good comfort, rise; he called thee. And he, casting away his garment rose, and came to Jesus. And Jesus answered and said unto him, What wilt thou that I should do unto thee? The blind man said unto him, Lord, that I might receive my sight. And Jesus said unto him, Go thy way; thy faith hath made thee whole. And immediately he received his sight, and followed Jesus in the way" (Mark 10:46–52).

When Bartimaeus pressed in to Jesus, it got his attention. Jesus stood still. People may say to you things like—I don't want to hear about Jesus, or keep that Jesus stuff in church. Yet the moment you press in despite opposition, you have the full attention of Jesus. He will ask you the same question. *What is it you want me to do for you?* Then you tell him and release your faith and you will get the same results. It was faith that brought the grace of God, for Jesus said, "thy faith hath made thee whole."

If you will believe God at his word, you will get the same result, for Jesus is no respecter of persons and is the same yesterday, today, and forever. Let's see how Jesus dealt with blind men in Matthew, chapter 9.

"And when he came into the house, the blind men came to him: and Jesus saith unto them, Believe ye that I am able to do this? They said unto him, Yea, Lord. Then touched he their eyes, saying, According to your faith be it unto you. And their eyes were opened; and Jesus straitly charged them, saying, see that no man know it" (Matt. 9:28–30).

Jesus is asking the same question today. *Do you believe that I am able to do this?* You must believe that Jesus is willing and able to heal you, not just other people like Billy Graham. Jesus is the same today and no respecter of persons. It works the same way today. Jesus tells you that he is willing to heal you. You must have faith. Then you tell him that you want to be healed, what specifically you want him to do, and that you believe he is able to do it. Then by faith, you receive the healing that is available to whosoever will receive it.

"And when the men of that place had knowledge of him, they sent out into all that country round about, and brought unto him all that were diseased; And besought him that they might only touch the hem of his garment: and as many as touched were made perfectly whole" (Matt. 14:35–36).

God desires greatly for us to receive our healing. Jesus took thirty-nine stripes on his back so that we could be healed. Jesus will never say no to your healing. If Jesus wanted to say no, he wouldn't have had to take one stripe. He didn't take stripes on his back to say no, he took the stripes so that he could say, *YES*!

Jesus Christ, the Son of God, came to earth to take punishment for our sins.

"For he hath made him to be sin for us, who knew no sin; that we might be made the righteousness of God in him"(2 Cor. 5:21).

It was the punishment that we deserved. But if we trust in Jesus, instead of paying for our sins, we are born again and set free from the curse of the law.

"Christ hath redeemed us from the curse of the law, being made a curse for us: for it is written, Cursed is every one that hangeth on a tree: That the blessing of Abraham might come on the Gentiles through Jesus Christ; that we might receive the promise of the Spirit through faith" (Gal. 3:13–14).

Jesus has set us free from the curse of the law. The curse of sin brings not only sickness, but also poverty and eternal separation from God. The blood of Jesus has brought us healing, prosperity, and eternal life with Jesus.

"Yet a little while, and the world seeth me no more; but ye see me: because I live, ye shall live also" (John 14:19).

God had a solution for healing of our physical bodies. "He sent his word, and healed them, and delivered them from their destructions" (Ps. 107:20).

Jesus, the living Word, not only shed his blood for the healing of our bodies, but for the healing of every area of our lives. Jesus healed all who were oppressed of the Devil. The Devil oppresses us in more areas than just our physical body. If you are oppressed in any way, Jesus has shed his divine blood so that you can be

healed by faith. Jesus healed all who had diverse diseases and torments. The innocent, perfect, pure blood of God has been shed to offer you healing for whatever kind of oppression your enemy, the Devil, has brought to you.
Before Jesus was crucified, blood flowed from the crown of thorns that we might have a sound mind.

"And they stripped him, and they put on him a scarlet robe. And when they had platted a crown of thorns, they put it on his head, and a reed in his right hand: and they bowed the knee before him, and mocked him, saying, Hail, King of the Jews! And they spit upon him, and took the reed, and smote him on the head. And after that they had mocked him, they took the robe off from him, and put his own raiment on him, and led him away to crucify him" (Matt. 27:28–31).

If you are oppressed in your mind with confusion or fear, you can put on the mind of Christ by faith.

"Let this mind be in you, which was also in Christ Jesus" (Phil. 2:5)

"For God hath not given us the spirit of fear; but of power, and of love, and of a sound mind" (2 Tim. 1:7).

If you are anxious or fearful about something you must face in the future, then by faith let Jesus set you free, because his blood flowed that we might be free from anxiety. Jesus knew the great ordeal he would have to go through. He knew he was going to take the greatest beating of all time and then be crucified. He had to go through the greatest anxiety so that we could be set free from it. He was under such great stress that blood flowed from his sweat glands.

"And he came out, and went, as he was wont, to the mount of Olives; and his disciples also followed him. And when he was at the place, he said unto them, Pray that ye enter not into temptation. And he was withdrawn from them about a stone's cast, and kneeled down, and prayed, saying, Father, if thou be willing, remove this cup from me: nevertheless not my will, but thine, be done. And there appeared an angel unto him from heaven, strengthening him. And being in agony he prayed more earnestly; and his sweat was as it were great drops of blood falling to the ground" (Luke 22:39–44).

We don't have to worry about our future or what lies ahead, for the blood of Jesus has made a way of victory. The degree to which we make Jesus the source of our supply is the degree to which to which we can live with out anxiety.

"Be careful for nothing; but in every thing by prayer and supplication with thanksgiving, let your requests be made known unto God" (Phil. 4:6).

"Casting all your care upon him; for he careth for you" (1 Peter 5:7).

The Lord Jesus is Jehovah Jireh—the God who sees ahead and makes provision. Trust in the Lord. He is smarter than we are and he knows the future. He supplies for our needs in advance. Whatever your future needs might be, God has already commanded the provision to be there. We just have to obey. When the drought came, God instructed Elijah to go where God had already commanded the provision to be. It's still the same way today.

"Get thee hence, and turn thee eastward, and hide thyself by the brook Cherith, that is before Jordan. And it shall be that thou shall drink of the brook; and I have commanded the ravens to feed thee there"(1 Kings 17:3–4).

Later, when the brook dried up, God had already commanded Elijah's future provision.

"And the word of the Lord came unto him, saying, Arise, get thee to Zarephath, which belongeth to Zidon, and dwell there; behold, I have commanded a widow woman there to sustain thee" (1Kings 17:8–9)

Before the fall of man, Adam and Eve lived in paradise. This was God's original plan for man and he hasn't changed his mind. Life on earth was like life in heaven. Why? Adam and Eve never worried or were anxious about anything. That's why it was paradise. They never had thoughts like "how will I pay for college for my children" or "what if I fail in my marriage" or "what if I lose my job." They simply trusted God.

Because we can enter into a blood covenant with God Almighty, through the blood of Jesus, we too can live on earth like it's paradise. We can bring heaven down to touch the earth. We simply make God our source of supply for every area in our lives.

"But my God shall supply all your need according to his riches in glory by Christ Jesus" (Phil. 4:19).

Not only will God supply your needs, but he will supply all your wants and desires that he has put into your heart.

"Therefore I say unto you, What things soever ye desire, when you pray, believe that ye receive them, and ye shall have them" (Mark 11:24).

Yes, I'm talking about desires that go well beyond just your needs. However, we must do things God's way and receive the things we desire by faith and according to God's timing. God is not like a genie in a bottle. It is through faith and patience that we receive the promise. God himself has put the desires in your heart to have good things of the kingdom. So don't be afraid. It is his good pleasure to give you the kingdom.

Life is not as complicated as most people think. If you are in covenant with Jesus, all you have to do is please him and everything else takes care of itself. Trust in God, make him your source of supply, and by faith you can live on earth like it is in heaven.

"Therefore take no thought, saying, What shall we eat? Or, Wherewithal shall we be clothed? (for after all these things do the Gentiles seek) for your heavenly Father knoweth that ye have need of all these things. But seek ye first the Kingdom of God and his righteousness; and all these things shall be added unto you" (Matt. 6:31–33).

Those who have entered into a blood covenant with God by being born again by the spirit of God have eternal life and can walk in health and prosper.

"Beloved, I wish above all things that thou mayest prosper and be in health, even as thy soul prospereth." (3 John v.2).

Remember, God does not automatically heal and prosper you. We have to call upon his promises in the name of Jesus. Every good thing comes to us through Jesus. The only qualification to receive from the Father is that we know his Son. We have to have made Jesus our Lord and Savior.

Every one needs Jesus because our sins have separated us from a holy God. There is not anyone who has not told a lie or committed a sin. God, however, is holy and cannot fellowship with sin. So he sent his son, Jesus, to be a man and pay for our sins that we might have the righteousness of God.

Jesus took on our sins, and by faith, we can receive the exchange of his righteousness and therefore boldly enter into the throne of grace. It's not based on what we have done but what Jesus has done for us. If you will receive Jesus, you will never have to be ashamed again, for Jesus will not be ashamed of you.

"For both he that sanctifieth and they who are sanctified are all of one: for which cause he is not ashamed to call them brethren" (Heb. 2:11).

Because of the sin of Adam, we stand condemned until we receive Jesus by faith. Jesus did not come into the world to condemn the world but to set us free from the condemnation we are already in. It is a free gift of God. We simply receive it by faith.

"Therefore as by the offence of one judgement came upon all men to condemnation: even so by the righteousness of one the free gift came upon all men unto justification of life. For as by one man's disobedience many were made sinners, so by the obedience of one shall many be made righteous. Moreover the law entered, that the offence might abound. But where sin abounded, grace did much more abound: That as sin hath reigned unto death, even so might grace reign through righteousness unto eternal life by Jesus Christ our Lord" (Rom. 5:18–21).

If you have never received Jesus into your heart, but you would like to, then pray this prayer and mean it in your heart. You will inherit eternal life and can begin walking in your inheritance by receiving provision and health on this earth in the name of Jesus.

Lord Jesus, I am a sinner. Forgive me of my sins, come into my heart, and make me brand new. Wash me clean in your precious blood. I confess you as my Lord and Savior and I will serve you all the days of my life. Jesus, thank you for saving me. I thank you that I am now a child of God and my name is written in Heaven. I thank you that I now can call upon your name for healing and provision. Help me to make you my source of supply for every area of my life. AMEN

Chapter 7

What About Tribulations?

If God is always good, does that mean we won't have to go through tribulations? God is indeed always good, but as long as you are on the earth, you will have to go through tribulations. Jesus told us that. Everyone likes the promises of God, right? Below are listed three promises of God.

"In the world ye shall have tribulation: but be of good cheer; I have overcome the world" (John 16:33b).

"Many are the afflictions of the righteous: but the LORD delivereth him out of them all (Ps. 34:19).

"Beloved, think it not strange concerning the fiery trial which is to try you, as though some strange thing happened unto you: But rejoice, inasmuch as ye are partakers of Christ's sufferings; that, when his glory shall be revealed, ye may be glad also with exceeding joy (1 Pet. 4:12–13).

As Jesus said, in *this* world we shall have tribulations. Once we are in heaven, our troubles will be over. There are no tribulations in heaven, there are no afflictions in heaven, and there are no fiery trials in heaven. That's good news.

Each one of the above Scriptures taken as a whole is good news to the believer. There is nothing that we can go through that Jesus has not already faced and won the victory for us. Remember, we do not have to receive or accept anything that Jesus has redeemed us from. We should resist it and take authority over it. Jesus redeemed us from the curse of the law, which includes sickness and poverty. That means we have spiritual authority over them. Praise the Lord! However, there are cares and problems and troubles that we have to face and deal with on the earth. The Bible refers to them as thorns or tares.

"Another parable put he forth unto them, saying, The kingdom of heaven is likened unto a man which sowed good seed in his field: But while men slept, his enemy came and sowed tares among the wheat, and went his way. But when the blade was sprung up, and brought forth fruit, then appeared the tares also. So the servants of the householder came and said unto him, Sir, didst not thou sow good seed in thy field? from whence then hath it tares? He said unto them, an enemy hath done this" (Matt. 13: 24–28a).

Our Enemy brings the tares and thorns. The Enemy's purpose for these cares of the world is explained to us in Mark chapter 4.

"And these are they which are sown among thorns; such as hear the word, And the cares of this world, and the deceitfulness of riches, and the lusts of other things entering in, choke the word, and it becometh unfruitful" (Mark 4: 18–19).

The purpose of thorns and tares is to get our eyes off Jesus and the Word as we put them on our problems, thereby making the Word unfruitful in our lives. Remember when Peter was walking on water in Matthew chapter 14? He was walking in the supernatural on the word of God until he got his eyes on the storm (his problem).

"And he said, Come. And when Peter was come down out of the ship, he walked on the water, to go to Jesus. But when he saw the wind boisterous, he was afraid; and beginning to sink, he cried, saying, Lord, save me. And immediately Jesus stretched forth his hand, and caught him, and said unto him, O thou of little faith, wherefore didst thou doubt?" (Matt.14:29–31).

The storms of life come from the Enemy also. If Jesus brings the storms then he won't rebuke storms. He rebukes storms because he is not the author of the storms.

"And there arose a great storm of wind, and the waves beat into the ship, so that it was now full. And he was in the hinder part of the ship, asleep on a pillow: and they awake him, and say unto him, Master, carest thou not that we perish? And he arose, and rebuked the wind, and said unto the sea, Peace, be still. And the wind ceased, and there was a great calm. And he said unto them, Why are ye so fearful? how is it that ye have no faith? And they feared exceedingly, and said one to another, What manner of man is this, that even the wind and the sea obey him?" (Mark 4: 37–41).

Jesus won't bring a storm and then rebuke it just as he won't make someone sick then heal him. He won't lead us into temptation then deliver us from evil. God is not double minded. As we discussed in chapter 6, Jesus won't divide his kingdom. The Devil brings the storms and Jesus or his joint heirs rebuke them.

Many people think that God sent Paul a thorn in the flesh. This is not true. Why would God want us to take our eyes off Jesus and the promises of God? Satan wants us to take our eyes off what we are going to and put them on what we are going through. Jesus wants us to keep our eyes on what we are going to and not on what we are going through. Jesus said to the disciples, "let us go over to the other side." The Devil doesn't want you to make it to the other side, so he brings storms to make you quit. We should rebuke the storms as Jesus did. The Bible clearly says that it was a messenger of Satan who gave Paul a thorn in the flesh.

"And lest I should be exalted above measure through the abundance of the revelations, there was given to me a thorn in the flesh, the messenger of Satan to buffet me, lest I should be exalted above measure. For this thing I besought the Lord thrice, that it might depart from me. And he said unto me, My grace is sufficient for thee: for my strength is made perfect in weakness. Most gladly therefore will I rather glory in my infirmities, that the power of Christ may rest upon me. Therefore I take pleasure in infirmities, in reproaches, in necessities, in persecutions, in distresses for Christ's sake: for when I am weak, then am I strong" (2 Cor. 12:7–10).

This was not a sickness that God refused to heal. Paul was not blind or nearsighted. We know that Paul was healed of his blindness three days after his Damascus experience while he was still called Saul.

"And Ananias went his way, and entered into the house; and putting his hands on him said, Brother Saul, the Lord, even Jesus, that appeared unto thee in the way as thou camest, hath sent me, that thou mightest receive thy sight, and be filled with the Holy Ghost. And immediately there fell from his eyes as it had been scales: and he received sight forthwith, and arose, and was baptized" (Acts 9: 17–18).

Thorns represent the cares of this world or tribulations. Paul went through many tribulations. God was not refusing deliverance for Paul or for you. He won't make it so you don't have tribulations, because the only way to do that is take you out of this world. He does say that his grace is sufficient for us. To receive grace we must show God some faith.

Paul responded to God and used his faith mightily. Despite great demonic opposition he accomplished great things for the Lord by looking at what he was going to and not at what he was going through. He kept his eyes on Jesus, who brought him victoriously through every storm, until he referred to the tribulations in his life as "light afflictions."

Storms come from the Enemy. They are not acts of God as described by insurance companies. A storm is defined as a disturbance in the air. Who is the prince of the power of the air? Our Enemy, the Devil is.

"Wherein in time past ye walked according to the course of this world, according to the prince of the power of the air, the spirit that now worketh in the children of disobedience" (Eph. 20:2).

Our Enemy uses storms to bring fear into our lives, and the Bible says that fear hath torment. In fact, the Spanish word for storm is *tormenta*. The Devil is the tormenter. God always wants us in faith and never wants us in fear.

"For God hath not given us the spirit of fear; but of power, and of love, and of a sound mind" (2 Tim 1:7).

The cares of this world and the storms of life are designed by the Devil to choke the Word, make it unfruitful, and make us afraid to keep going forward in the things of God. Jesus wants us to take dominion over storms and sicknesses. If he didn't want us to exercise dominion over natural things, even including gravity, he wouldn't have said to Peter to come when he invited him to walk on water. Since Jesus is always the same and no respecter of persons, he wants us to come into the supernatural realm by taking dominion over the things of this world and the world system.

The apostle Paul went through a lot of tribulations and storms, yet he triumphed over them and instructed us to keep our eyes on Jesus in the middle of a trial.

"Looking unto Jesus the author and finisher of our faith; who for the joy that was set before him endured the cross, despising the shame, and is set down at the right hand of the throne of God" Heb. 12: 2).

The Devil wants us to walk by sight and not by faith, but God wants us to walk by faith and not by sight. God is not bringing bad things into our life. God will not make you sick; he will not sow tares and thorns in your life; he will not send storms, and he will not tempt you.

"Let no man say when he is tempted, I am tempted of God: for God cannot be tempted with evil, neither tempteth he any man" (James 1:13).

Again, God doesn't send sickness or storms or sow tares or deliver thorns or tempt us, and we should take dominion over these things in the name of Jesus as we look toward what we are going to in the Lord. Well, does that mean that everything that makes us uncomfortable comes from the Devil? No, God won't send bad things, but sometimes, for our good, he may put us in a place where we are uncomfortable. It will be a place where we must stretch our faith. God won't tempt us to do wrong, but he will test his people, and he will do that in only one area.

Because he put the kingdom principle of sowing and reaping in the earth, God has a right to test us in the area of provision. He can do that for he has allowed us to test him or prove him in that area of our lives.

"Bring ye all the tithes into the storehouse, that there may be meat in mine house, and prove me now herewith, saith the LORD of hosts, if I will not open you the windows of heaven, and pour you out a blessing, that there shall not be room enough to receive it" (Mal. 3: 10).

God proves us just as we prove him. The greatest example of that was when the children of Israel crossed the wilderness to enter into the Promised Land. They had to be proved first so their faithfulness would enable them to enjoy and be blessed when walking in the land of the promises of God.

"And thou shalt remember all the way which the LORD thy God led thee these forty years in the wilderness, to humble thee, and to prove thee, to know what was in thine heart, whether thou wouldest keep his commandments, or no"(Deut. 8:2).

The trip into the Promised Land would have been a short journey if only they would have passed the test right away. God is a good educator. He won't pass you to the next level unless you pass the test. Current educators should take a lesson from God. The most prominent thing that I see in this period of learning that should have been very short is that God doesn't take things away from us to teach us.

Notice that God's people had fresh, nourishing food every day. They had fresh water every day, even if it had to come out of a rock. They had fellowship with each other and experienced the presence of God. Their clothes and shoes were like new every day and never wore out, even after forty years. They had protection with the clouds by day and the pillar of fire by night. They witnessed the supernatural provision of God every day. Not one person ever got sick, not even one. Oh yes, they even had great wealth with a large amount of gold because they spoiled the Egyptians. Notice God took none of these things away from them.

He wants us to learn from him willingly because we honor his word and his voice. The children of Israel did squander much of their gold by forming a golden calf. That was their own disobedient act, which was certainly not directed by God. If we will obey God and be faithful with our tithes and offerings, then we are proved as we prove God and we can move into our promised land. As long as we are on this earth, we will always have to sow seeds beyond our perceived abilities in order to go to the next level with God. As we do, God will teach us and we'll experience an increase not a loss, for God doesn't have to take good things from us to teach us. If God doesn't want us to have something, then we shouldn't want it, because all good things come from God.

"Every good gift and every perfect gift is from above, and cometh down from the Father of lights, with whom is no variableness, neither shadow of turning" (James 1:17).

All the children of Israel had to learn was three things. Before entering the Promised Land, they had to learn that God is the source of all provision. They had to learn that God is a good provider. They had to learn to follow God wherever he leads them for he will always take his children to a good place where there is provision. We should learn these things too. Anything that comes from God is to bless us. He wants to lead us into a good place. There is no need to be afraid, no matter how things look.

"When thou passest through the waters, I will be with thee; and through the rivers, they shall not overflow thee: when thou walkest through the fire, thou shalt not be burned; neither shall the flame kindle upon thee" (Isa. 43:2).

If we trust God, we will not be drowned, and we will not be burned, because Jesus overcame all tribulations for us. The crown of thorns representing tribulations caused blood to flow to bring victory for us. It brought us victory over tribulations because the blood has freed our minds to think about the joy that is set before us rather than what we are going through. That is why we can rejoice in the fiery trial because promotion is always our reward when we come through the fire.

We cast our cares, or our thorns, upon Jesus because he cares for us. We are not made to carry heavy burdens. They can weigh us down and destroy us. We must give them to God and let him handle them. He knows what to do when we don't.

"Come unto me, all ye that labour and are heavy laden, and I will give you rest. Take my yoke upon you, and learn of me; for I am meek and lowly in heart: and ye shall find rest unto your souls. For my yoke is easy, and my burden is light" (Matt. 11:28–30).

Promotion always comes when we make it through the fiery trial. We can rejoice because we can make it through and blessings and promotion are waiting at the end of this short journey! We don't have to look at our problems if we keep looking unto Jesus for the joy or promotion set before us.

God has designed us to be reward motivated. God does not make mistakes. He designed us that way and knows what he is doing. If it is wrong to be reward motivated then Jesus was wrong. Let's look at Hebrews 12:2 again as well as Hebrews 11:6.

"Looking unto Jesus the author and finisher of our faith; who for the joy that was set before him endured the cross, despising the shame, and is set down at the right hand of the throne of God" Heb. 12:2).

"But without faith it is impossible to please him: for he that cometh to God must believe that he is, and that he is a rewarder of them that diligently seek him" (Heb. 11:6).

Jesus was motivated by looking to his reward and promotion after enduring the cross. We can endure the crucifying of our flesh if we keep looking unto Jesus and his reward of promotion. Jesus endured the most and therefore got the greatest promotion. Our promotion will come for us just like it did for Jesus, but we must know that it is coming and look forward to it. We don't want to go through it for nothing. We should be like Jesus and receive our promotion by faith.

"Let this mind be in you, which was also in Christ Jesus: Who, being in the form of God, thought it not robbery to be equal with God: But made himself of no reputation, and took upon him the form of a servant, and was made in the likeness of men: And being found in fashion as a man, he humbled himself, and became obedient unto death, even the death of the cross. Wherefore God also hath highly exalted him, and given him a name which is above every name: That at the name of Jesus every knee should bow, of things in heaven, and things in earth, and things under the earth;

And that every tongue should confess that Jesus Christ is Lord, to the glory of God the Father" (Phil. 2: 5–11).

God's greatest victories came from God's people who understood that God is a rewarder. Among many others, Paul and Moses believed for their reward.

"Brethren, I count not myself to have apprehended: but this one thing I do, forgetting those things which are behind, and reaching forth unto those things which are before, I press toward the mark for the prize of the high calling of God in Christ Jesus" (Phil. 3:13–14).

"By faith Moses, when he was come to years, refused to be called the son of Pharaoh's daughter; Choosing rather to suffer affliction with the people of God, than to enjoy the pleasures of sin for a season; Esteeming the reproach of Christ greater riches than the treasures in Egypt: for he had respect unto the recompence of the reward. By faith he forsook Egypt, not fearing the wrath of the king: for he endured, as seeing him who is invisible" (Heb. 11: 24–27).

I have very good news. We don't have to wait until we are in heaven to enjoy our rewards. We already have our inheritance if we are born again. If God didn't want us to walk in it now, then he wouldn't have given it to us now.

"Then Peter began to say unto him, Lo, we have left all, and have followed thee. And Jesus answered and said, Verily I say unto you, There is no man that hath left house, or brethren, or sisters, or father, or mother, or wife, or children, or lands, for my sake, and the gospel's, But he shall receive an hundredfold <u>now in this time</u>, houses, and brethren, and sisters, and mothers, and children, and lands, with persecutions; and in the world to come eternal life" Mark (10: 28–30).

We start receiving our rewards in this time because God put sowing and reaping into the earth. There is one catch. Because there is a devil present in this world, our rewards come with persecutions. Sadly, the persecutions often come from religious men who are ignorant of God's desire to bless and reward his people. If we are receiving God's very best, a hundred-fold return, we will have no problem standing up to and overcoming persecutions. Praise the Lord!

As a preview to chapter 9, it's time to change the way we think and the way we talk. God doesn't complain about what he doesn't have if he doesn't have what he wants. He speaks what he wants until what he has becomes what he wants. We should do the same thing. Let's quit talking to God about how big our mountain is and start talking to our mountain about how big our God is. When we are in the fire, God has a way of escape, which is for our good to promote us and to help us reach others.

The promotion brings more influence in people's lives so we can bring the goodness of God to them for God's glory. We are blessed to be a blessing. We are delivered to be a deliverer. We are healed to be a healer. We are set free to set people free. We are lifted up to lift others up. We are encouraged to encourage others. And most of all, we are saved to be soul winners.

Here are some examples of fiery trials resulting in promotion. Let's start with the three Hebrew children Shadrach, Meshach, and Abed-nego. The Word of God gives us the account of their amazing experience in the fiery furnace.

"Nebuchadnezzar spake and said unto them, Is it true, O Shadrach, Meshach, and Abed-nego, do not ye serve my gods, nor worship the golden image which I have set up? Now if ye be ready that at what time ye hear the sound of the cornet, flute, harp, sackbut, psaltery, and dulcimer, and all kinds of musick, ye fall down and worship the image which I have made; well: but if ye worship not, ye shall be cast the same hour into the midst of a burning fiery furnace; and who is that God that shall deliver you out of my hands? Shadrach, Meshach, and Abed-nego, answered and said to the king, O Nebuchadnezzar, we are not careful to answer thee in this matter. If it be so, our God whom we serve is able to deliver us from the burning fiery furnace, and he will deliver us out of thine hand, O king. But if not, be it known unto thee, O king, that we will not serve thy gods, nor worship the golden image which thou hast set up. Then was Nebuchadnezzar full of fury, and the form of his visage was changed against Shadrach, Meshach, and Abed-nego: therefore he spake, and commanded that they should heat the furnace one seven times more than it was wont to be heated. And he commanded the most mighty men that were in his army to bind Shadrach, Meshach, and Abed-nego, and to cast them into the burning fiery furnace. Then these men were bound in their coats, their hosen, and their hats, and their other garments, and were cast into the midst of the burning fiery furnace. Therefore because the king's commandment was urgent, and the furnace exceeding hot, the flame of the fire slew those men that took up Shadrach, Meshach, and Abed-nego. And these three men, Shadrach, Meshach, and Abed-nego, fell down bound into the midst of the burning fiery furnace. Then Nebuchadnezzar the king was astonied, and rose up in haste, and spake, and said unto his counsellers, Did not we cast three men bound into the midst of the fire? They answered and said unto the king, True, O king. He answered and said, Lo, I see four men loose, walking in the midst of the fire, and they have no hurt; and the form of the fourth is like the Son of God. Then Nebuchadnezzar came near to the mouth of the burning fiery furnace, and spake, and said, Shadrach, Meshach, and Abed-nego, ye servants of the most high God, come forth, and come hither. Then Shadrach, Meshach, and Abed-nego, came forth of the midst of the fire. And the princes, governors, and captains, and the king's counsellers, being gathered together, saw these men, upon whose bodies the fire had no power, nor was an hair of their head singed, neither were their coats changed, nor the smell of fire had passed on them. Then Nebuchadnezzar spake, and said, Blessed be the God of Shadrach, Meshach, and Abed-nego, who hath sent his angel, and delivered his servants that trusted in him, and have changed the king's word, and yielded their bodies, that they might not serve nor worship any god, except their own God. Therefore I make a decree, That every people, nation, and language, which speak any thing amiss against the God of Shadrach, Meshach, and Abed-nego, shall be cut in pieces, and their houses shall be made a dunghill: because there is no other God that can deliver after this sort. Then the king promoted Shadrach, Meshach, and Abed-nego, in the province of Babylon" (Dan. 3: 14–30).

Before they went into the fire, the three men were bound up from persecution. They were loosed, even in the midst of the fire, because Jesus was with them. When they came out, they were promoted. When you come out of the fire without even the smell of smoke on you, it will impress and convert even people of great influence, who will then use their influence for good instead of evil. What is the first thing that happened to them when they came out of the fire? They were promoted by the king. The king of kings will promote us too when we come out of the fire.

Notice that four men were in the fire but only three men came out. Jesus is still in the fire, waiting in advance to protect you so that when you trust him you will not be burned. Not only were the three Hebrew children promoted, but so was the kingdom of God. The same thing happened to Daniel when he refused to stop praying. The Devil sent persecution, but God sent protection, personal advancement, and kingdom advancement.

"Then the king commanded, and they brought Daniel, and cast him into the den of lions. Now the king spake and said unto Daniel, Thy God whom thou servest continually, he will deliver thee. And a stone was brought and laid upon the mouth of the den; and the king sealed it with his own signet, and with the signet of his lords; that the purpose might not be changed concerning Daniel. Then the king went to his palace, and passed the night fasting: neither were instruments of musick brought before him: and his sleep went from him. Then the king arose very early in the morning, and went in haste unto the den of lions. And when he came to the den, he cried with a lamentable voice unto Daniel: and the king spake and said to Daniel, O Daniel, servant of the living God, is thy God, whom thou servest continually, able to deliver thee from the lions? Then said Daniel unto the king, O king, live for ever. My God hath sent his angel, and hath shut the lions' mouths, that they have not hurt me: forasmuch as before him innocency was found in me; and also before thee, O king, have I done no hurt. Then was the king exceeding glad for him, and commanded that they should take Daniel up out of the den. So Daniel was taken up out of the den, and no manner of hurt was found upon him, because he believed in his God. And the king commanded, and they brought those men which had accused Daniel, and they cast them into the den of lions, them, their children, and their wives; and the lions had the mastery of them, and brake all their bones in pieces or ever they came at the bottom of the den. Then king Darius wrote unto all people, nations, and languages, that dwell in all the earth; Peace be multiplied unto you. I make a decree, That in every dominion of my kingdom men tremble and fear before the God of Daniel: for he is the living God, and stedfast for ever, and his kingdom that which shall not be destroyed, and his dominion shall be even unto the end. He delivereth and rescueth, and he worketh signs and wonders in heaven and in earth, who hath delivered Daniel from the power of the lions. So this Daniel prospered in the reign of Darius, and in the reign of Cyrus the Persian" (Dan. 6: 16–28).

There is a reason to rejoice when the fiery trial comes to try us. Let's look at one more example. I have picked out a few verses to look at concerning Joseph, Israel's son, after his brothers sold him into slavery.

"And the name of the second called he Ephraim: For God hath caused me to be fruitful in the land of my affliction" (Gen. 41:52).

"Now therefore be not grieved, nor angry with yourselves, that ye sold me hither: for God did send me before you to preserve life. For these two years hath the famine been in the land: and yet there are five years, in the which there shall neither be earing nor harvest. And God sent me before you to preserve you a posterity in the earth, and to save your lives by a great deliverance. So now it was not you that sent me hither, but God: and he hath made me a father to Pharaoh, and lord of all his house, and a ruler throughout all the land of Egypt" (Gen. 45:5–8).

"But as for you, ye thought evil against me; but God meant it unto good, to bring to pass, as it is this day, to save much people alive" (Gen. 50:20).

If we will trust God, the persecution the Enemy sends will backfire on him and we will end up the victor. We must be reward motivated and keep looking at what we are going to and not what we are going through. We must call the things that are not as though they are, and the victory will be ours. There will be a day when we will have no more thorns. We will receive real crowns. It will be beyond what we can dream.

"But as it is written, Eye hath not seen, nor ear heard, neither have entered into the heart of man, the things which God hath prepared for them that love him" (1 Cor. 2: 9).

Anyone can rejoice and be faithful when things are going good. God is looking for people like Joseph who can produce fruit even in the land of affliction so lives can be saved. God is looking for people who know God will deliver them, for they know God is a rewarder of them that diligently seek him. He wants you to be faithful and trustworthy, even in a fire or storm, so you can enjoy all the blessings and benefits of God that come through promotion. If you will live your life like that, you will be so blessed, and one day you will hear the most wonderful words that a man, woman, boy or girl can ever hear from Jesus: "His lord said unto him, Well done, good and faithful servant; thou hast been faithful over a few things, I will make thee ruler over many things: enter thou into the joy of thy lord" (Matt. 25: 23).

Chapter 8

How to Recover What the Devil Has Stolen

God has truly made a way for us to dwell under the shadow of his wing and receive continuous protection. He has made a way that by faith we can walk through the waters and the fire and not be drowned or burned. We have learned that God works all things, even terrible acts of our Enemy, to our good if we will trust him. All that is good news, yet each one of us has faced or will face loss in this world. I don't know of anyone who has never stepped out of the hiding place of God at some time. Additionally, we can suffer loss due to persecution because of what we have done right in obedience to God. Elijah's brook dried up because of his obedience to declare that it wouldn't rain until King Ahab repented.

We need to know what to do when we suffer loss in this world. If we trust God with the knowledge of what we learn in this chapter, we will recover what we lose plus the spoils, or God will give us something better to replace it. I don't know how he does it, but he is the God of the impossible. God is smarter than we are and he knows the future. We have to trust him to decide if we should recover exactly what we lose, plus the spoils, or recover something different but better than we had before. In either case, we come out ahead when we trust God. For purposes of our study, we will call both cases a recovery of what the Devil has stolen, and leave the rest to God.

Let's discuss the situation where God replaces what we have lost with a different but better plan. That is what God did for Joshua and the children of Israel in Joshua chapter 1.

"Now after the death of Moses the servant of the LORD it came to pass, that the LORD spake unto Joshua the son of Nun, Moses' minister, saying, Moses my servant is dead; now therefore arise, go over this Jordan, thou, and all this people, unto the land which I do give to them, even to the children of Israel. Every place that the sole of your foot shall tread upon, that have I given unto you, as I said unto Moses. From the wilderness and this Lebanon even unto the great river, the river Euphrates, all the land of the Hittites, and unto the great sea toward the going down of the sun, shall be your coast. There shall not any man be able to stand before thee all the days of thy life: as I was with Moses, so I will be with thee: I will not fail thee, nor forsake thee. Be strong and of a good courage: for unto this people shalt thou divide for an inheritance the land, which I sware unto their fathers to give them. Only be thou strong and very courageous, that thou mayest observe to do according to all the law, which Moses my servant commanded thee: turn not from it to the right hand or to the left, that thou mayest prosper whithersoever thou goest. This book of the law shall not depart out of thy mouth; but thou shalt meditate therein day and night, that thou mayest observe to do according to all that is written therein: for then thou shalt make thy way prosperous, and then thou shalt have good success" (Josh. 1: 1–8).

God was telling Joshua to stop crying over the death of Moses (stop crying over things you have lost in the past). In the previous chapter, we focused on looking at what you're going to instead of what you are going through. Sometimes we can't see what we are going to because we keep looking at what we have *been through*. We have to let go of the past.
"Brethren, I count not myself to have apprehended: but this one thing I do, forgetting those things which are behind, and reaching forth unto those things which are before, I press toward the mark

for the prize of the high calling of God in Christ Jesus" (Phil. 3:13–14).

Until we stop crying, we can't move into our new territory. It's not wrong to cry, but there is a time to stop crying and move on. God told Joshua to forget past losses so he could lead God's people into the Promised Land. If we will obey God and more toward the place he has for us, God will give us every place on which we set our feet.

God gave Joshua limits as described in verse 4. The Lord has given us a place, the right location, as discussed in chapter 1. We can't do more than what we are called to do. We can't be everywhere and we can't be all things to all people. We should be faithful right where we are—where God has placed us. If we can't love the people around us, how can we love the nations of the world?

"If a man say, I love God, and hateth his brother, he is a liar: for he that loveth not his brother whom he hath seen, how can he love God whom he hath not seen?" (1 John 4:20).

If we won't pray for our own families or our neighbors, then how can we pray for missionaries? As we do what God has called us to do, where God has called us to do it, no man will be able to stand against us. As soon as we start walking in the area God gave us, as soon as we step on it, the protection of God will come, the power of God will come, the provision of God will come, and the blessing of God will come.

Many times God restores exactly what we have lost, plus more. That *more* is the spoil taken from the Enemy. This is what David experienced after he left Ziklag. We will use that example to reveal seven supernatural steps to recover what the Devil has stolen.

Remember, recovery could be the same as what you lost plus the spoils or something different but better. It may not seem better at first, but in the end you will see the good hand of God. Let's read the story of David at Ziklag.

"And it came to pass, when David and his men were come to Ziklag on the third day, that the Amalekites had invaded the south, and Ziklag, and smitten Ziklag, and burned it with fire; And had taken the women captives, that were therein: they slew not any, either great or small, but carried them away, and went on their way. So David and his men came to the city, and, behold, it was burned with fire; and their wives, and their sons, and their daughters, were taken captives. Then David and the people that were with him lifted up their voice and wept, until they had no more power to weep. And David's two wives were taken captives, Ahinoam the Jezreelitess, and Abigail the wife of Nabal the Carmelite. And David was greatly distressed; for the people spake of stoning him, because the soul of all the people was grieved, every man for his sons and for his daughters: but David encouraged himself in the LORD his God. And David said to Abiathar the priest, Ahimelech's son, I pray thee, bring me hither the ephod. And Abiathar brought thither the ephod to David. And David inquired at the LORD, saying, Shall I pursue after this troop? shall I overtake them? And he answered him, Pursue: for thou shalt surely overtake them, and without fail recover all. So David went, he and the six hundred men that were with him, and came to the brook Besor, where those that were left behind stayed. But David pursued, he and four hundred men: for two hundred abode behind, which were so faint that they could not go over the brook Besor. And they found an Egyptian in the field, and brought him to David, and gave him bread, and he did eat; and they made him drink water; And they gave him a piece of a cake of figs, and two clusters of raisins: and when he had eaten, his spirit came again to him: for he had eaten no bread, nor drunk any water, three days and three nights. And David said unto him, To whom belongest thou? and whence art thou? And he said, I am a young man of Egypt, servant to an Amalekite; and my master left me, because three days agone I fell sick. We made an invasion upon the south of the Cherethites, and upon the coast which belongeth to Judah, and upon the south of Caleb; and we burned Ziklag with fire. And David said to him, Canst thou bring me down to this company? And he said, Swear unto me by God, that thou wilt neither kill me, nor deliver me into the hands of my master, and I will bring thee down to this company. And when he had brought him down, behold, they were spread abroad upon all the earth, eating and drinking, and dancing, because of all the great spoil that they had taken out of the land of the Philistines, and out of the land of Judah. And David smote them from the twilight even unto the evening of the next day: and there escaped not a man of them, save four hundred young men, which rode upon camels, and fled. And David recovered all that the Amalekites had carried away: and David rescued his two wives. And there was nothing lacking to them, neither small nor great, neither sons nor daughters, neither spoil, nor any thing that they had taken to them: David recovered all. And David took all the flocks and the herds, which they drave before those other cattle, and said, This is David's spoil" (1 Sam. 30: 1–20).

I don't think any of us have ever lost as much as David did. He lost all his family, all of his possessions, and then the men were talking about stoning him. At that point, David had no one but the Lord. There was no one to even encourage him, so David encouraged *himself* in the Lord. Sometimes we have no one around to encourage us. We have to encourage ourselves. David took the first step.

1. <u>Encourage yourself in the Lord</u>

In verse 6 we are told that David encouraged himself in the Lord. I'm sure he reminded himself of all the times that God had come through for him and how God never failed him when he put his trust in God. He probably thought of the times that God protected him, even when he had done wrong. He thought of how God had strengthened him to defeat the lion and the bear. He remembered how Goliath, as big as he was, fell because he used a spear and sword, but David used the name of the Lord. David reflected on the promises of God and the faithfulness of God. Even when there is no one to encourage us, we can encourage ourselves in the Lord. As we do, hope begins to rise up on the inside of us, and we are on our way to recovering what the Devil has stolen.

2. <u>Praise and worship the Lord</u>

In verse 7, David called for the linen ephod. An ephod is what the priest wore to minister to God. God has made us kings and priests.

"And hath made us kings and priests unto God and his Father" (Rev. 1: 6a).

David was wearing his ephod when he danced and leaped in joy before the Lord as he brought the ark back to God's people.

"And it was so, that when they that bare the ark of the LORD had gone six paces, he sacrificed oxen and fatlings. And David danced before the LORD with all his might; and David was girded with a linen ephod. So David and all the house of Israel brought up the ark of the LORD with shouting, and with the sound of the trumpet. And as the ark of the LORD came into the city of David, Michal Saul's daughter looked through a window, and saw king David leaping and dancing before the LORD; and she despised him in her heart. And they brought in the ark of the LORD, and set it in his place, in the midst of the tabernacle that David had pitched for it: and David offered burnt offerings and peace offerings before the LORD. And as soon as David had made an end of offering burnt offerings and peace offerings, he blessed the people in the name of the LORD of hosts. And he dealt among all the people, even among the whole multitude of Israel, as well to the women as men, to every one a cake of bread, and a good piece of flesh, and a flagon of wine. So all the people departed every one to his house. Then David returned to bless his household. And Michal the daughter of Saul came out to meet David, and said, How glorious was the king of Israel to day, who uncovered himself to day in the eyes of the handmaids of his servants, as one of the vain fellows shamelessly uncovereth himself! And David said unto Michal, It was before the LORD, which chose me before thy father, and before all his house, to appoint me ruler over the people of the LORD, over Israel: therefore will I play before the LORD.] And I will yet be more vile than thus, and will be base in mine own sight: and of the maidservants which thou hast spoken of, of them shall I be had in honour" (2 Sam 6: 13–22).

After we're encouraged, we praise the Lord and give sacrifices to the Lord. We bless others. We focus on the greatness of God and that there is nothing too hard for him. We see how big God is and then the task of recovery seems small. It's about this time that the tide begins to turn. The Devil starts to sweat, and he is now afraid of what we can do with our faith.

3. <u>Inquire of the Lord</u>

In verse 8, David inquired of the Lord. He asked the Lord if he would recover all, and the Lord said that without fail he would recover all. Since God never changes and is no respecter of persons, his answer to our inquiry is always that we shall recover all without fail. Praise the Lord!

4. Get into agreement and don't come out

David had 400 men that went with him, but 200 stayed behind. Remember how they all cried until they had no more strength to cry? Not everybody will be in agreement with you. Some will not go with you or support you, but that is all right. It's more important how much you are in agreement than how many are in agreement. Not everyone will agree with you, so find some faithful people who will agree with you for full recovery. Let them help you control what comes out of your mouth. Speak full recovery and stop crying over the loss. David's recovery didn't begin until the crying stopped. Again, it's not wrong to cry, but crying didn't help David and his men, and it won't help you. Find faith people and agree together for complete victory.

5. Identify the enemy

This is where most Christians miss it and therefore fail to recover all. In fact, if you fail to identify the enemy, things will get worse instead of better. People are not our enemy. If we come against people, the Devil will have more opportunities to steal from us. David identified his enemy in verses 13–14. He found out that the Amalekites had burned Ziklag with fire and stolen his family and belongings. We can only recover what was stolen from the person who has stolen from us. The Devil is our enemy and he is the one who steals from us.

"The thief cometh not, but for to steal, and to kill, and to destroy" (John 10: 10a).

Command the Enemy to give back what he has stolen. We need to know that he is afraid of the Jesus in us. We should use the name of Jesus and let God's power do the work.

"Recompense to no man evil for evil. Provide things honest in the sight of all men. If it be possible, as much as lieth in you, live peaceably with all men. Dearly beloved, avenge not yourselves, but rather give place unto wrath: for it is written, Vengeance is mine; I will repay, saith the Lord. Therefore if thine enemy hunger, feed him; if he thirst, give him drink: for in so doing thou shalt heap coals of fire on his head. Be not overcome of evil, but overcome evil with good" (Rom. 12: 17–21).

God's Word instructs us not to come against people. We should love people, even those who harm us, but we should show no mercy to the Devil and his forces. When the Enemy steals from us, we should make him pay. People are not our enemy.
"For we wrestle not against flesh and blood, but against principalities, against powers, against the rulers of the darkness of this world, against spiritual wickedness in high places" (Eph. 6: 12).

6. <u>Don't quit until you see the victory</u>

In verse 17, David smote the Amalekites. They were the identified enemy. The Amalekites always represent the enemies of God. The Bible says that David smote them from twilight to the evening of the next day. David and his men were tired. They had cried until they had no more power to weep. Then they mounted up and found the Amalekites. They were already exhausted before the battle began. They persevered because God had said that they would recover all. Even when you're tired, don't quit. You can't lose, because God has said to us in 1 Samuel 30: 8 that we shall recover all without fail. The only way we can lose is if we quit.

"And let us not be weary in well doing: for in due season we shall reap, if we faint not" (Gal. 6: 9).

It takes a decision on our part not to quit. Anyone can decide not to quit. It doesn't take any special talent, ability or gifting. Anyone can have the victory over the Enemy simply by not quitting.

7. Take the spoil

In verses 19–21, we see that David not only recovered all, but he also took the spoil. This is supposed to be a normal consequence for God's people. The children of Israel took spoil from the Egyptians when they left Egypt. God's people took the spoil of the children of Ammon and Moab and the inhabitants of Seir.
"And when Jehoshaphat and his people came to take away the spoil of them, they found among them in abundance both riches with the dead bodies, and precious jewels, which they stripped off for themselves, more than they could carry away: and they were three days in gathering of the spoil, it was so much" (2 Chron. 20: 25).

Command the spoils from the Enemy and expect to receive them. The spoils are ours because we are children of God. Make the Devil pay and make him think twice about messing with someone who understands the promise of the spoil. Remember, spoils may come in the form of something better.

Chapter 9

Changing Our Thinking

A long time truism from the Robert Burns poem *To a Mouse* accurately reflects the situation in our lives when our thinking differs from God's. Even though we think we have thought of everything and covered every contingency, "the best laid plans of mice and men often go awry." Reality sets in as we see our best-laid plans go up in the proverbial puff of smoke.

Without the Word of God, our natural mind is flawed. Our thinking is backward from God's thinking unless our minds are renewed by the Word of God. The thoughts of our carnal mind war against and are completely opposite from the thoughts of God. Below is a comparison of the thinking of man's natural mind versus the thinking of the mind of God.

The Natural Mind Says	God Says
Exalt yourself to get to the top.	Humble yourself then I will exalt you.
Show me and I'll believe you.	Believe me and I will show you.
First come, first served.	The first will be last and the last will be first.
What you don't know won't hurt you.	My people are destroyed for what they don't know.

The Natural Mind Says	God Says
It's better to receive than to give.	It's more blessed to give than to receive.
Great people get served.	The greatest is the one who serves.
You have to live before you can die.	You have to die before you can live.
I'll believe it when I see it.	You'll see it when you believe it.
Sticks and stones may break my bones but words will never harm me.	The power of death and life is in our words.
If I could understand the Bible I'd believe it.	If you'd believe the Bible you would understand it.
The way to increase is to take.	The way to increase is to give.
If I had it, I'd give.	If you'd give, you'd have it.
If I could find intimacy I'd make a commitment.	If you would commit, you would find intimacy.

Let's look at the last thought. People go from partner to partner searching for intimacy thinking that if they find it, they will make a commitment. With that thinking, they will never find it.

Intimacy only comes after you make a commitment. If we would just think more like our Daddy, we would lead much happier lives. Proverbs 14:12 and 16:25 both say the exact same thing.

"There is a way that seemeth right unto a man, but the end thereof are the ways of death" (Prov. 16:25 and Prov. 14:12).

There are many times in the New Testament when Old Testament Scriptures are quoted and thus appear twice in the Bible. This is not the case here. It must be very important to God that we get this message. What seems right to man brings failure, curses, sickness, poverty, and death. What seems right to God brings success, blessings, health, abundance, and life.

How you ever heard the expression called stinkin' thinkin'? Stinking thinking is thinking with the natural mind. The Word gives us a mental picture of stinking thinking.

"Why should ye be stricken any more? ye will revolt more and more: the whole head is sick, and the whole heart faint. From the sole of the foot even unto the head there is no soundness in it; but wounds, and bruises, and putrefying sores: they have not been closed, neither bound up, neither mollified with ointment" (Isa. 1:5–6).

There is no soundness in the human head. Without the thoughts of God, our heads are full of wounds, bruises, and putrefying sores that have not been tended to. The book of Isaiah tells us that our ways are not his ways and our thoughts are not his thoughts. Thank God that he thinks differently than we do. If what we think is different from God, then know this–he is right and we are wrong. We are the ones who have to change, not God.

Jesus walked the earth as a man and committed no sin, made every decision perfectly, and walked in perfect success and obedience to his heavenly Father. Jesus gave us his name, his word, his authority, his anointing and the Holy Ghost. He gave us all the things he used to walk perfectly. Yet, even with all of these wonderful resources and gifts, we still fail and make wrong decisions continually. What makes the difference? The difference is that his knowledge and thoughts were perfect.

Our minds have to be renewed. We are first of this world and then we are born again into the kingdom of God. But we still try to operate with the thinking of this world, and we fail. Jesus is first of the kingdom of God, was born into this world, and operated with the thinking and knowledge of the kingdom of God. Therefore, he was perfect in every way.

"And be not conformed to this world: but be ye transformed by the renewing of your mind, that ye may prove what is that good, and acceptable, and perfect, will of God" (Rom. 12:2).

"Let this mind be in you, which was also in Christ Jesus" (Phil. 2: 5).

The apostle Paul instructs us to put on the mind of Christ. If our thinking starts to change, we will change.

"For as he thinketh in his heart, so is he" (Prov. 23: 7a).

They way we think and the knowledge of the goodness of God is the key to the way we live because we are what we think. We can either think like man and fail or think like God and have success. When we think differently, we will talk differently.

"For out of the abundance of the heart the mouth speaketh" (Matt. 12: 34b).

What we think in our heart will come out of our mouth. It's just like a tube of toothpaste. When pressure is applied, the contents come out. Sometimes God will allow a little pressure so we can see what is in our heart by what comes out of our mouth. We must be careful what we speak, because what we speak sets our life and we speak what we think.

"A man shall be satisfied with good by the fruit of his mouth" (Prov. 12:14a).

"A man's belly shall be satisfied with the fruit of his mouth; and with the increase of his lips shall he be filled. Death and life are in the power of the tongue: and they that love it shall eat the fruit thereof" (Prov. 18: 20–21).

If you start to think like God, you will begin to talk like God. God talks differently than man. God uses the same creative power he has given us to manifest in the natural what he has believed in his heart. As children of God who are made in the image of God, we too have creative power with our words. We should operate as our heavenly Father to speak with our mouths what we believe in our hearts, so that what we believe might be manifest in the natural for the glory of God.

"(As it is written, I have made thee a father of many nations,) before him whom he believed, even God, who quickeneth the dead, and calleth those things which be not as though they were" (Rom. 4:17).

God created the world with his words and we create our world with our words. That's why we should think in our hearts like God thinks, because what is in our heart will come out of our mouth and what comes out of our mouth will create our world.

If what we speak determines who we are, but we speak what we think in our hearts, then it is easy to see why the Bible says in Proverbs 23: 7 that we are what we think in our hearts. We need to know the goodness of God so we can think in our hearts the truth of who God really is and therefore who we really are. We should know that God has good things for us, we can call them into being, and know they are ours even before we see them.

If we think like God, we will talk like God. If we talk like God, we will walk like God. If we walk like God, we will live like God on this earth as God intended from the start.

"Be ye therefore perfect, even as your Father which is in heaven is perfect" (Matt. 5: 48).

To be perfect or mature like our Father, it has to start with thinking like God and knowing who he is, what he is like, and how he thinks, especially how he thinks about us. As we discussed earlier, God is always thinking good thoughts about us. God has designed us to live like him on the earth since we are made in his image.

We are to rule and reign and be the head, not the tail—above only and not beneath. We should walk in that to such a degree that people will say that our God must be the one true God. Then we can more easily lead people from darkness into his marvelous light.

It starts by deciding to believe the Word. Then comes the understanding. Serving God is not as hard as religion has made it out to be. It is not a bunch of impossible dos and don'ts. All God is really asking us to do is believe him. If we will believe that what he says is true, we will seek him with all our hearts, and then everything good will follow.

"But seek ye first the kingdom of God, and his righteousness; and all these things shall be added unto you" (Matt. 6: 33).

God has told us that the way we change or are transformed into his likeness is through the renewing of our minds. We start out with a carnal mind that thinks like man. If we do nothing or just let things happen, we will not automatically be transformed, even if we are born again. Our minds have to be renewed. It will take effort on our part. We must not only read and hear God's Word; we must love the Word and meditate upon it all day long. If we do this, God will lead us to victory and keep us in a safe place.

"O how love I thy law! it is my meditation all the day. Thou through thy commandments hast made me wiser than mine enemies: for they are ever with me. I have more understanding than all my teachers: for thy testimonies are my meditation. I understand more than the ancients, because I keep thy precepts. I have refrained my feet from every evil way, that I might keep thy word. I have not departed from thy judgments: for thou hast taught me. How sweet are thy words unto my taste! yea, sweeter than honey to my mouth! Through thy precepts I get understanding: therefore I hate every false way. Thy word is a lamp unto my feet, and a light unto my path" (Ps. 119: 97–105).

"This book of the law shall not depart out of thy mouth; but thou shalt meditate therein day and night, that thou mayest observe to do according to all that is written therein: for then thou shalt make thy way prosperous, and then thou shalt have good success" (Josh. 1: 8).

"This I say therefore, and testify in the Lord, that ye henceforth walk not as other Gentiles walk, in the vanity of their mind, Having the understanding darkened, being alienated from the life of God through the ignorance that is in them, because of the blindness of their heart: Who being past feeling have given themselves over unto lasciviousness, to work all uncleanness with greediness. But ye have not so learned Christ; If so be that ye have heard him, and have been taught by him, as the truth is in Jesus: That ye put off concerning the former conversation the old man, which is corrupt according to the deceitful lusts; And be renewed in the spirit of your mind; And that ye put on the new man, which after God is created in righteousness and true holiness" (Eph. 4: 17–24).

We can change our thinking about who we are and who God is. We can understand that we are citizens of heaven, even though we live on the earth.

"But God, who is rich in mercy, for his great love wherewith he loved us, Even when we were dead in sins, hath quickened us together with Christ, (by grace ye are saved;) And hath raised us up together, and made us sit together in heavenly places in Christ Jesus" (Eph. 2: 4–6).

If we are transformed to live like God on the earth because we renew our minds, then we will have the same motives as Jesus to go about doing good, healing all who are oppressed of the Devil, and seeking to save those that are lost. Without the knowledge of the goodness of God, we can be tormented and even destroyed. But the knowledge of the goodness of God can give us everything good, including the life of God.

"According as his divine power hath given unto us all things that pertain unto life and godliness, through the knowledge of him that hath called us to glory and virtue" (2 Peter 1: 3).

Chapter 10

Introduction to the Book of Job

We can learn a lot about the goodness of God from the book of Job if we think correctly as we study it. The book of Job rivals the book of Revelation as the most incorrectly taught book in the Bible. It requires some introductory teaching before we begin.

Let's look again in the first chapter of the book of Colossians.

"For this cause we also, since the day we heard it, do not cease to pray for you, and to desire that ye might be filled with the knowledge of his will in all wisdom and spiritual understanding; That ye might walk worthy of the Lord unto all pleasing, being fruitful in every good work, and increasing in the knowledge of God" (Col. 1: 9–10).

This is what God desires for you. He wants you to produce fruit in everything you do. He wants everything you do to please him while you increase in the knowledge of his goodness and therefore produce more fruit and please him even more. It is also my desire for you to be filled with all spiritual understanding and knowledge of the goodness of God.

Many people misquote 2 Timothy 3:16 by saying or believing that all Scripture is inspired of God. What it says is that all Scripture *is given* by inspiration of God.

"All scripture is given by inspiration of God, and is profitable for doctrine, for reproof, for correction, for instruction in righteousness" (2 Tim. 3: 16).

Again, all Scripture is *given by* inspiration of God, but not all Scripture is inspired of God. The recording of what happened was given by inspiration of God. Some events recorded in the Bible were authored by people who were not even present at the time the events occurred, but we can count on the accuracy because they were given what to write by the inspiration of God. This does not mean that the person in any given account who committed an act or made a statement was necessarily inspired of God to do or say what they did.

When the serpent in the book of Genesis said, "thou shalt not surely die," he was not inspired of God to say that. The writer (Moses) was inspired of God to write the truth that the serpent said those words. Annias and Saphira were not inspired of God to say they gave all the proceeds of the sale of their land to the church, but God inspired Luke to write down the truth of what happened.

The Pharisees said this about Jesus:

"But when the Pharisees heard it, they said, This fellow doth not cast out devils, but by Beelzebub the prince of the devils" (Matt. 12: 24).

The Pharisees were not inspired by God to say that lie. It was a demonic spirit of pride that was behind it. However, God inspired Matthew to record it exactly as it happened. Do we want to follow their example? Do we want the Pharisees to shape our perception of God? Of course not, so please be advised that Job also did a lot of talking—saying things that were not true, and he was not inspired of God to do so. We don't want his words of ignorance to shape our perception of God just because we find them in the Bible. This precept should cause us to follow the advice of Paul to Timothy.

"Study to shew thyself approved unto God, a workman that needeth not to be ashamed, rightly dividing the word of truth" (2 Tim. 2:15).

Here are some other examples of statements made by people and found in the Bible that were not inspired of God. We should not use these as examples of how we should think and talk. For the sake of brevity, I will paraphrase what they said.

Jezebel – Take Naboth's land from him

Korah – Moses is not God's man to lead us

Lucifer – I will exalt myself

King Nebuchadnezzar – Look at all I've accomplished

Satan – Jesus, throw yourself down and worship me

Goliath – I defy the armies of Israel

Don't you think that heathens would speak differently if they knew the God of Israel loved them and wanted to show kindness to them? Remember how the speeches of King Nebuchadnezzar and King Darius changed when they saw the miracles done for the three Hebrew children and Daniel. This problem of wrong thinking and thus wrong speaking is not just a problem for the heathens, but also for God's people.

The cause of the problem is the same for us. We need our minds totally renewed. The more our minds are renewed, the less of this we do. But until our minds are totally renewed our mouths can still get us in trouble. A person can be saved and still think and speak like a lost man. Even some of God's best servants needed to work on renewing their minds, and so do we. Here are some examples of God's people who spoke wrong and did wrong. Are their actions our examples? But brother David, you say, it's in the Bible. Well, so is the Devil, and he's not my example. Again, for the sake of brevity, I will paraphrase.

King David – Put Uriah on the front lines

Peter – I don't know the man

Abraham – Sarah is my sister

Joseph's brothers – Father, Joseph is dead, an animal ate him

We have to study to rightly divide the word of truth. Let Scripture interpret Scripture rather than you interpret Scripture. If you interpret it, you will be ashamed. Just because someone in the Bible says something, it doesn't necessarily make it right. Not every word spoken in the Bible reflects right thinking or godly wisdom. The Devil speaks in the Bible, and he is father of all lies.

Here are some additional things we need to know before we study the book of Job:

1. Job did not have the full revelation of God and God's character that is revealed to us in the New Testament.

2. This limited revelation caused Job to say things about God that were not true. It was true that he said them, but he was not inspired of God to say what he said.

3. Satan caused all of Job's problems. God blessed Job and gave him twice as much as he had before.

Job was just ignorant. He was nearly destroyed for his lack of knowledge about God, but God did everything he could to bless him and get his life turned around. The Devil sent some of Job's ignorant friends to speak more lies to Job. God, on the other hand, sent his anointed man, Elihu, but when Job didn't listen to him, God himself showed up and spoke directly to Job.

God allowed bad things to happen to Job because Job was free to be ignorant of God, free to be in fear, and free to be self-righteous. God didn't put any bad things on Job. During Job's entire ordeal, God was trying to work with Job so he would choose God and be blessed. Job finally came around when he started thinking right about what God was really like. God is good and his mercy endures forever.

Again, it was Satan that caused all of Job's problems, but it was God who blessed him with twice as much. Job was just ignorant of the goodness of God. He was thinking *que sera, sera*. Job was nearly destroyed for his lack of knowledge about God.

Chapter 11

The Trouble with Job's Thinking

Why did devastation come to Job? Not understanding the answer to that question is one of the biggest hindrances keeping us from walking in our full inheritance. Most of the lack of understanding that people have comes from bad teaching. Please understand, I'm not against preachers who have taught the book of Job incorrectly. The vast majority of them are sincere and trying to help. They are just sincerely wrong, and their lack of knowledge can bring you down.

Many wonderful ministers have wonderful testimonies, know more Bible than I do, and have helped and blessed many people. I don't want to pass judgment on anybody; I just need to get the truth out. Pray for your pastor or the preachers you listen to because what they say can greatly affect your life.

For example, it wasn't the giants that kept the children of Israel out the Promised Land, it was the negative preachers. Twelve spies came back and preached a message to the people. The Bible says that ten preached an evil report, and the people believed them over the two prosperity preachers. All twelve of them saw the same thing, yet they drew different conclusions. The evil report was fear based and reported on the giants. The advice was: let's stay the same. Joshua and Caleb's report was faith based and said: let's walk in the promises of God, even though there are giants, because God has spoken. What you hear preached is important because faith comes by hearing.

I want you to receive good teaching about Job that lines up with the whole counsel of God. Beyond that, I have to stand up for my God. I know he doesn't need me to do that for him, but I want to. I want to please him, and I want you blessed and not cursed. My natural father was a great man. He was a kind and generous man. He loved his family and cared about people. If people falsely accused him of doing bad things, I wouldn't believe them. I would stand up and say that I know my father and he would never do that. You don't know him like I do. Doesn't our heavenly Father deserve the same from his children?

Now we are ready to study the book of Job. Let's start in chapter 1.

"Now there was a day when the sons of God came to present themselves before the LORD, and Satan came also among them. And the LORD said unto Satan, Whence comest thou? Then Satan answered the LORD, and said, From going to and fro in the earth, and from walking up and down in it. And the LORD said unto Satan, Hast thou considered my servant Job, that there is none like him in the earth, a perfect and an upright man, one that feareth God, and escheweth evil?" (Job 1: 6–8).

Here's the normal teaching you'll get on that passage. I'm warning you upfront that this is wrong. Here it is: "Well, God just wanted to see how much Job could take, how much he would endure and still love God." Or, "God will use the Devil to discipline us."

It's true that God disciplines his children, but he doesn't use his archenemy to do it. If your children need discipline, do you do it yourself, or do you get your enemy to do it?

I'm reminded of what I heard one of my favorite preachers, Gerald Davis, say when preaching from the book of Job. He related the notion of God using the Devil to discipline his kids to a parent calling the warden at the prison. I can't remember exactly what he said, and I'm sure I have embellished it for dramatic purposes. But the phone call went something like this:

Father: Hello, Warden.

Warden: What can I do for you?

Father: I have a son who needs some correction. Who do you have in there that that can punish him? I want the meanest man you have, the one who has committed the most heinous crimes, someone with no mercy.

Warden: I have a couple of murderers, will they do?

Father: Will they show any mercy?

Warden: They might.

Father: I want someone with no mercy.

Warden: I know. How about Charles Manson?

Father: That's more like it. Now you're talking. Allow him to destroy everything my son has and mark him up from head to toe, but don't let him kill him.

Would we do that to our children? Why would we think that God would do that with his? God doesn't want his archenemy, the most hardened criminal who possesses no love or mercy, a thief who comes to steal, kill and destroy, to discipline his kids. God will discipline and correct his children, but he handles it personally just as I discipline my own children, because I want to do it with love and get good results.

Imagine a father driving in a car with rowdy young children in the back seat. The father turns around and thumps the children on the head and it really hurts them. That act may have changed their behaviors, but it didn't change their hearts. God knows how to discipline us so it not only changes our behaviors but it changes our hearts, so that the behavior then takes care of itself.

The book of Job is in the Bible to be an example and a blessing to us. Would you rather read about Job's problems and learn that way, or go through it yourself to learn? I would rather read and let the Holy Ghost teach me. This book shows us how we get into trouble, and it shows us how to get out of trouble. Both lessons are valuable to know. That is why the book of Job is *not* in the Bible to show how much a man can take. It is in the Bible to show us that we can trust a good God, even when we find ourselves in a mess that we brought on ourselves.

Sometimes we just don't know why we are in the mess that we are in. Sometimes, like Elijah, we are in a mess because of our own faith ministry. We can also get in trouble because we sow bad seed. We speak fear words and it opens the door for the Enemy. We also can have bad things happen just because we are in the world, and this world is a place of tribulation.

In this world we are going to have tribulation, and if you can't figure out why, don't panic, because it's all right. The way out from contact with trouble, the way out from a bad seed sown, and the way out from an attack of the Devil because you're doing good is the same way out for all of them.

We call on the name of the Lord. We trust in him, we run into his arms and tell him that we are going to do things his way. We examine ourselves. If we're doing wrong, we quit it and start doing it right. The things we're doing right, we keep on doing right and declare the goodness of God and the mighty works of the Lord. We find a promise in the Word and then we believe it in our heart and speak it in the name of Jesus. We trust God and say to him, Lord, what is my part to do? We don't want to do God's part. We just want to do our part. Now God will let us try to do his part if we get stubborn enough. He has given us a free will. But if we try to do God's part, we are on our own and destined to fail. I don't want to be on my own. I want Daddy fighting the battle for me. I just want to do what he wants me to do.

We already have the victory if we just trust in his goodness. We can go through the waters, and we'll not be drowned. We can go through the fire and we'll not be burned. If we trust God, we'll come out of the fire without even the smell of smoke. What does that mean? It means that when we are delivered and people look at us, they will never know that we were in a fire unless we tell them.

The answer to every problem or need that we will ever have has already been placed in us when we are born again. All we have to do is speak it as God did when he made the world. This earth was in God, and he spoke and it manifested in the natural. God framed his world with what he spoke and we frame our world with what we speak. Everything we need is in us and we have to speak it for it to manifest in the natural.

"According as his divine power hath given unto us all things that pertain unto life and godliness, through the knowledge of him that hath called us to glory and virtue" (2 Peter 1: 3).

"Behold, the kingdom of God is within you" (Luke 17: 21b).

God hath given, (past tense), unto us everything that pertains to life (natural) and godliness (spiritual). It's in us and we can birth it by believing in our heart and speaking with our mouth.

Our focus should not be on why things happened, because we don't know everything and we can't see into people's hearts. We should always seek wisdom concerning God's principles but with the understanding that there are some things only God knows. His focus is not on placing blame but on healing those who are oppressed. That should be our focus as well.

"Then Satan answered the LORD, and said, Doth Job fear God for nought? Hast not thou made an hedge about him, and about his house, and about all that he hath on every side? thou hast blessed the work of his hands, and his substance is increased in the land. But put forth thine hand now, and touch all that he hath, and he will curse thee to thy face. And the LORD said unto Satan, Behold, all that he hath is in thy power; only upon himself put not forth thine hand. So Satan went forth from the presence of the LORD" (Job 1: 9–12).

Verses 9–11 show what happens when we are in the hands of God. In the hands of God, everything was blessed. Satan couldn't touch Job and Satan complained about it. In verse 12 we find that all Job had was in Satan's hands, but Job himself was still in God's hands. God didn't put Job's possessions in Satan's hands, he just acknowledged that they were already there. They were under Satan's power and authority.

Something happened that caused what Job had to get out of God's hands and get into the hands of Satan. Yet, Job himself was in God's hands and Satan couldn't touch him, just as he couldn't touch what he had before when there was a hedge of protection all around him. If Satan could have gotten to Job's belongings, he wouldn't have complained. The hedge around what Job had somehow became broken.

"And the LORD said unto Satan, Behold, he is in thine hand; but save his life" (Job 2:6).

How did what Job had, then later Job's body, get into Satan's hands? Let me make this clear. People who love God and serve Jesus can, in certain areas of their life, place themselves into the Devil's hands. Let me explain.

When we are born again, we receive protection over our life, our body and our possessions as we walk under the shadow of the Almighty according to the promises in Psalm 91. God puts a hedge of protection around us. Sometimes we walk out of that protection, don't we? That is why we're to *dwell* there to receive the promises. When we leave that place to do our own thing, we can find trouble and suffer loss. We will accomplish so much more for the kingdom, personally and in every other goal that we have, if we just dwell in the secret place.

God puts a hedge of protection around us when we are born again and we no longer belong to the Devil. We belong to our Father God who is good and whose mercies endure forever. When we belong to God, all that we have belongs to God because it's his as we are in covenant. He protects us because we belong to him.

Let's look at our tithe as an example. We belong to God and he says that the first tenth of our increase is his. If we don't believe him and trust him, and therefore are not faithful with our tithe, we open the door to the Devil. Our hedge is broken and God cannot protect our money because now it is not in God's hands. We have released it to Satan. He has an open door to steal it. That happens when we say that we don't believe what that preacher is saying. It's not about what the preacher is saying it's about what God has said.

The root cause of disobedience in the tithe is the same root cause for all disobedience–fear. The following is how our mind works when we let fear enter in. Fear can only exist when we doubt the goodness of God.

"If I do what God says, it's not going to work. How am I going to have more money if I give to God? I'm going to do it my own way."

If we act on that fear and withhold the tithe, then there is a hedge broken in our finances and the Devil can enter and put your finances in his hands. If we are obedient to bring the whole tithe into the storehouse, and the Devil approaches your finances, he will be rebuffed by God's hedge of protection.

There are certain areas in our lives in which we are doing well because our minds are renewed in those areas. Yet, there might be other areas that we haven't turned over to God, simply because we want to hold on to them. Most people have some area in their life that, even when their minds are much renewed in other areas, they still want to do it their way. The bottom line is that, in that area, they are afraid to trust God.

The Devil can't do anything to you in the absence of fear and God can't do anything for you in the absence of faith. God needs faith to bless you and the Devil needs fear to curse you. Let's do it God's way. I want my whole life, marriage, business, ministry, etc. inside the protective hedge of the Lord. Sometimes, I mess up. Thank God, he will always take me back with his arms open wide, showing me he wants to take care of his little boy.

As we run to his arms, we are no longer in the Devil's hands. The Devil has no legal right to invade God's territory. He does it as a thief. The thief cannot penetrate God's hedge.

"Submit yourselves therefore to God. Resist the devil, and he will flee from you" (James 4: 7).

We submit ourselves to God. That means we get under his protection. We resist the Devil by trusting God because we know God is always for good and always for us. Then the Devil must flee. If we call someone up and invite him to come over to our house, that would not qualify as resistance, would it? Sometimes we don't resist the Devil, in fact, we invite him in. How? We invite him by the words of our mouth. It's hard to resist someone when we've just invited him over.

Sometimes we give the Devil permission to come over even if it's in ignorance. God wants his people to know these things so we won't make that mistake through ignorance. God wants us to resist the Devil so he will have to flee from us.

This doesn't mean that we won't have trials, but it does mean that when we stand up to Satan with the knowledge of the goodness of God, he will have to flee. When the smoke clears, not even the smell of smoke will be on us.

We break our hedge of protection when we speak words of fear, giving the Devil permission to enter our lives. Remember the children of Israel crossing the wilderness. They said – Oh! that we would just die in this place – and they did. They received what they spoke. They didn't trust God and they didn't realize the power of their words. We need to know that God has given us power in our words, and that God lives inside of us. When we speak, it's the same as God speaking.

When God speaks, things happen. God said, "let there be light" and then there was light. If we keep believing something and speaking it over and over again, it is going to happen, whether it's good or bad. There have been times that I have brought problems into my life that I didn't have to go through because I kept speaking the wrong thing out of fear. There is no one who is exempt from that, and we need to be careful what comes out of our mouth.

It's awfully hard to speak fear words when we are in the shadow of God's wing. That is why we need to dwell there. Job broke down his own hedge.

"He that diggeth a pit shall fall into it; and whoso breaketh an hedge, a serpent shall bite him" (Eccl. 10:8).

Well, that's what happened. Job broke his hedge, a serpent came in and started to bite him. If someone bites hard enough and often enough, we call that devouring. That's what the Devil does. He goes around looking for a broken hedge, seeking whom he may devour. Guess whose hedge he is looking at the most? He is especially looking for a break in the hedge of someone who is serving God and operating under the anointing—someone whom

God is using to bring about miracles. As we serve the Lord, we have to be careful of our words and be on guard all the more of what we say.

Sometimes out of ignorance or we get tired or we are not thinking right, we give place to the Devil. The Bible says give no place to the Devil. If that happens, we should run to our Daddy. Job took too long to do that because he didn't know what God was really like.

"And his sons went and feasted in their houses, every one his day; and sent and called for their three sisters to eat and to drink with them. And it was so, when the days of their feasting were gone about, that Job sent and sanctified them, and rose up early in the morning, and offered burnt offerings according to the number of them all: for Job said, It may be that my sons have sinned, and cursed God in their hearts. Thus did Job continually" (Job 1: 4–5).

Job operated in fear over his children. He was in continual fear that something terrible would happen to them and it did. He not only thought it continually but he spoke it continually.

"For the thing which I greatly feared is come upon me, and that which I was afraid of is come unto me. I was not in safety, neither had I rest, neither was I quiet; yet trouble came" (Job 3: 25–26).

What came upon him was his loss and what came unto him were his boils. What he feared happened because he not only constantly worried about it (neither had I rest) but he constantly spoke of it (neither was I quiet). As a result, trouble came. It wasn't that he was just a little concerned, he greatly feared these things, he broke down his hedge with worry, and he didn't know to run to God. Due to his ignorance, Job thought God was doing it to him. He was thinking *que será, será*. Job needed to know the goodness of God.

We need to walk in faith instead of fear, because without fear the Devil is helpless. We need to guard against fear, for the just are meant to live by faith. We can't be in faith and fear at the same time. Let's walk by faith and not by sight. To worry, get depressed and carry burdens will never bring blessing. They will only produce what they are designed to produce–failure, problems and sickness.

"The fear of man bringeth a snare: but whoso putteth his trust in the LORD shall be safe" (Prov. 29:25).

Scriptures are given for our instruction. We don't want to do what Job did to get into defeat, but we should do what Job did to get into victory. We can use this book as instruction, and that's why God included these events in his Word. It's not there so people can bash God's name and bear false testimony against a loving God. Job got in to fear because he didn't trust God.

Job didn't trust God because of his lack of knowledge of who God really is. It's the same for you and me. Without knowledge of the goodness of God, we won't trust God. That's why I'm always talking about how good God is. This lack of knowledge caused Job to say things about God that were not true. Remember, it is true that he said those words, but some of his words he spoke do not line up with the truth of Scripture. Let Scripture interpret Scripture. Once Job became enlightened, he spoke right words as God himself confirms in chapter 42.

Let's read some of Job's words. Remember, <u>these words are wrong and spoken out of ignorance.</u>

"And said, Naked came I out of my mother's womb, and naked shall I return thither: the LORD gave, and the LORD hath taken away; blessed be the name of the LORD" (Job 1: 21).

Of course we will not return to our mother's womb. That should give us a clue that the rest of the sentence is without knowledge too. God will not divide his kingdom by giving and taking away. God gives us good gifts and the Devil tries to take them away. Notice Job ends his remarks by blessing the Lord. Job was a good man, but he was ignorant of the character of God. In the beginning of the book, he starts with a good attitude towards God. Later, because he thought God was bringing the devastation, Job became bitter in his heart and followed that up with self-righteousness. The same thing can happen to us with a lack of understanding of God's nature.

The next wrong statement of Job's is found below:

"If I had called, and he had answered me; yet would I not believe that he had hearkened unto my voice. For he breaketh me with a tempest, and multiplieth my wounds without cause. He will not suffer me to take my breath, but filleth me with bitterness" (Job 9: 16–18).

Job has falsely accused God. God can't give us bitterness because he doesn't have bitterness to give. God is love. He doesn't want his children carrying bitterness in their hearts against their heavenly Father. The Devil, who accuses God and us, offered bitterness to Job, and because of his ignorance, Job took it.

"Thine hands have made me and fashioned me together round about; yet thou dost destroy me" (Job 10: 8).

Let me remind you that these remarks are all wrong. Why would we let such foolish, ignorant remarks guide our theology? These words clearly violate the basics of Scripture. The Bible clearly tells us that it is the Devil or the thief that destroys. The Devil and God are complete opposites. Look at the words of Jesus:

"The thief cometh not, but for to steal, and to kill, and to destroy: I am come that they might have life, and that they might have it more abundantly" (John 10:10).

Here are some more false statements by Job:

"Though he slay me, yet will I trust in him: but I will maintain mine own ways before him" (Job 13: 15).

Job's lack of understanding has now taken him from false accusation to bitterness to self-righteousness. He head is so messed up that it reminds me of Isaiah 1:5. His whole head is sick. He is going to maintain his righteousness so God won't be justified for his mistreatment of Job. People quote this verse thinking that it is true and are ignorant to the fact they are falsely accusing God. They even include it in songs. They sing then cry and say, "Man, did we have church!" They had church all right, church for the Devil. We have to study to show ourselves approved. Jesus came to give you life, not slay you.

"How many are mine iniquities and sins? make me to know my transgression and my sin. Wherefore hidest thou thy face, and holdest me for thine enemy? Wilt thou break a leaf driven to and fro? and wilt thou pursue the dry stubble? For thou writest bitter things against me, and makest me to possess the iniquities of my youth" (Job 13:23–26).

Jesus, who is the express image of the Father, didn't come to bring condemnation but to forgive us. Condemnation is not of God. God is not writing down our iniquities, but is blotting them out.

"For God sent not his Son into the world to condemn the world; but that the world through him might be saved" (John 3:17).

"Blotting out the handwriting of ordinances that was against us, which was contrary to us, and took it out of the way, nailing it to his cross" (Col. 2 :14).

God does not want us to have a sin consciousness. He never has and he never will.
Once we are his, he wants to convict us of our righteousness—our righteousness in him, not our own righteousness.

"Have pity upon me, have pity upon me, O ye my friends; for the hand of God hath touched me" (Job 19:21).

Everything in God's hands is blessed. It was Satan who brought the boils to Job's body.

"So went Satan forth from the presence of the LORD, and smote Job with sore boils from the sole of his foot unto his crown" (Job 2: 7).

"Moreover Job continued his parable, and said, As God liveth, who hath taken away my judgment; and the Almighty, who hath vexed my soul; All the while my breath is in me, and the spirit of God is in my nostrils; My lips shall not speak wickedness, nor my tongue utter deceit. God forbid that I should justify you: till I die I will not remove mine integrity from me. My righteousness I hold fast, and will not let it go: my heart shall not reproach me so long as I live" (Job 27: 1–6).

This is so pitiful. Job thinks that his righteousness exceeds that of God's. God has done all these terrible things to him and he is not going to justify God's evil deeds. How will he keep God unjustified? He is going to hold fast to his own righteousness and his own integrity. In his mind, he is not going to mistreat God, even though God is mistreating him, because his integrity and righteousness is greater than God's.

Now it's time for God's response to Job's ranting. Even though Job is trashing him, God still loves Job and is doing everything he can to deliver him and bless him. Because Job has a free will, God cannot bless Job without his cooperation. So God sent an anointed preacher named Elihu to tell Job the truth. When that didn't work, God himself came to Job to speak directly to him. God loves us with an everlasting love.

Again, it is true that Job said all the things we read in Scripture, but he was not inspired of God to say them. Job was wrong and eventually God himself tells Job and us that Job was wrong. God sends Elihu to help Job straighten out his thinking.

"Wherefore, Job, I pray thee, hear my speeches, and hearken to all my words (Job 33:1).

"Surely thou hast spoken in mine hearing, and I have heard the voice of thy words, saying, I am clean without transgression, I am innocent; neither is there iniquity in me. Behold, he findeth occasions against me, he counteth me for his enemy, He putteth my feet in the stocks, he marketh all my paths. Behold, in this thou art not just: I will answer thee, that God is greater than man. Why dost thou strive against him? for he giveth not account of any of his matters" (Job 33:8–12).

"For Job hath said, I am righteous: and God hath taken away my judgment. Should I lie against my right? my wound is incurable without transgression. What man is like Job, who drinketh up scorning like water? Which goeth in company with the workers of iniquity, and walketh with wicked men. For he hath said, It profiteth a man nothing that he should delight himself with God. Therefore hearken unto me, ye men of understanding: far be it from God, that he should do wickedness; and from the Almighty, that he should commit iniquity. For the work of a man shall he render unto him, and cause every man to find according to his ways. Yea, surely God will not do wickedly, neither will the Almighty pervert judgment" (Job 34: 5–12).

Why did God say that Job was a perfect or mature and upright man that avoids evil? If he was so mature then why did devastation come to Job? Let me answer those questions with more questions. How do you talk about your children? Do you tell your enemy all your children's weaknesses? We must remember that God talks differently than man talks. God calls the things that are not as though they were. Job was not perfect, but God was speaking good things over him so that they would come to pass. Rejoice in the fact that even though we are not perfect our God is speaking good things over us so they will come to pass. We should do the same thing with our children. Don't speak their weaknesses over them but declare by faith that they can do all things through Christ who strengthens them.

We can't win if we strive against God. Why would we want to? God has good things for us. We don't need to depend on our own goodness; we depend upon the goodness of God, and then our works are good because we have no fear. God does not do wicked acts, but gave his life to set us free from it. God will not pervert judgment as Job has said. Elihu came to speak the truth of God. Elihu's discourse with Job continues.

"Elihu spake moreover, and said, Thinkest thou this to be right, that thou saidst, My righteousness is more than God'?" (Job 35:1–2).

"Therefore doth Job open his mouth in vain; he multiplieth words without knowledge" (Job 35:16).

Job's lack of knowledge of the goodness of God messed up his whole life. Why would anyone want to mimic Job's words? If you want to do that, wait and mimic his words from chapter 42 once God helps Job think and talk right.

"Touching the Almighty, we cannot find him out: he is excellent in power, and in judgment, and in plenty of justice: he will not afflict" (Job 36:23).

Elihu was a spokesman for God. We should listen to him as opposed to a bitter man who thinks his righteousness is more than God's. God will not afflict. It was the Enemy that took his children and struck his body because Job broke his hedge through ignorance of God.

"As the bird by wandering, as the swallow by flying, so the curse causeless shall not come" (Eccl. 26:2).

Elihu obeyed God, but Job's foolishness was stubborn. God did not give up on Job. Just as he does with you and me, God longed to deliver and bless Job. Unfortunately, God first had to talk straight with Job to turn around his thinking. God personally responded to the false statements that Job had made. God spoke to set the record straight. It was a great act of love. We have a wonderful heavenly Father. Let's see how he brought recovery to Job.

"Then the LORD answered Job out of the whirlwind, and said, Who is this that darkeneth counsel by words without knowledge? Gird up now thy loins like a man; for I will demand of thee, and answer thou me. Where wast thou when I laid the foundations of the earth? declare, if thou hast understanding" (Job 38: 1–4).

Job begins to see himself compared to God. He begins to see his righteousness next to God's.

"Moreover the LORD answered Job, and said, Shall he that contendeth with the Almighty instruct him? he that reproveth God, let him answer it. Then Job answered the LORD, and said, Behold, I am vile; what shall I answer thee? I will lay mine hand upon my mouth. Once have I spoken; but I will not answer: yea, twice; but I will proceed no further. Then answered the LORD unto Job out of the whirlwind, and said, Gird up thy loins now like a man: I will demand of thee, and declare thou unto me. Wilt thou also disannul my judgment? wilt thou condemn me, that thou mayest be righteous?" (Job 40: 1–8).

Here we see the reason that men want to blame a loving God for bad things. They do it so they can be righteous in their own eyes. It reminds me of Adam, after his first sin, when he blamed God because of the woman that God gave him. If people knew of the goodness of God we wouldn't need to cling to our own goodness, we would instead run to a loving, generous and forgiving God. God's correction worked and Job saw the truth. He repented and put himself back in the hands of God.

"Then Job answered the LORD, and said, I know that thou canst do every thing, and that no thought can be withholden from thee. Who is he that hideth counsel without knowledge? therefore have I uttered that I understood not; things too wonderful for me, which I knew not" (Job 42:1–3).

Don't take my word for it that Job's words before chapter 42 were all messed up. God's man Elihu said it, then God said it, and finally Job himself says it. He uttered things that he didn't understand.

"I have heard of thee by the hearing of the ear: but now mine eye seeth thee. Wherefore I abhor myself, and repent in dust and ashes. And it was so, that after the LORD had spoken these words unto Job, the LORD said to Eliphaz the Temanite, My wrath is kindled against thee, and against thy two friends: for ye have not spoken of me the thing that is right, as my servant Job hath. Therefore take unto you now seven bullocks and seven rams, and go to my servant Job, and offer up for yourselves a burnt offering; and my servant Job shall pray for you: for him will I accept: lest I deal with you after your folly, in that ye have not spoken of me the thing which is right, like my servant Job. So Eliphaz the Temanite and Bildad the Shuhite and Zophar the Naamathite went, and did according as the LORD commanded them: the LORD also accepted Job. And the LORD turned the captivity of Job, when he prayed for his friends: also the LORD gave Job twice as much as he had before" (Job 42: 5–10).

When Job's possessions and Job's body were in the hands of God, there was nothing but blessing. There was a hedge of protection around Job and the Devil could not penetrate it. Through Job's continual speaking of his fear came a break in the hedge around what he had and later a break in the hedge around his body. When Job changed his thinking, his life changed.

"So the LORD blessed the latter end of Job more than his beginning: for he had fourteen thousand sheep, and six thousand camels, and a thousand yoke of oxen, and a thousand she asses. He had also seven sons and three daughters. And he called the name of the first, Jemima; and the name of the second, Kezia; and the name of the third, Keren-happuch. And in all the land were no women found so fair as the daughters of Job: and their father gave them inheritance among their brethren. After this lived Job an hundred and forty years, and saw his sons, and his sons' sons, even four generations. So Job died, being old and full of days" (Job 42: 12–17).

The book of Job culminates with a disclosure of the wonderful results from Job's learning a lesson about the goodness of God. He never questions or doubts the goodness of God again, and we see the difference in his life. Accusing God brings nothing good and attracts the Devil to your life. Job goes from the figurative outhouse to the penthouse simply by changing the way he thought about God. Job no longer merely knew about God from what he heard from others, but he knew God from a personal encounter. His knowledge of the goodness of God brought him blessing and prosperity.

The right thinking of Job produced right talking. Job changed the way he talked about God. The Lord noticed the change. God said that Job was saying the right things about him. Job trashed God for 41 chapters but as soon as Job started talking right, God forgot all the harsh accusations Job had made. Even when Job's purpose was to keep his own righteousness, God forgave him and forgot all of Job's shortcomings when he proclaimed the goodness of God. Job knew he spoke wrong and said he should have laid his hand over his mouth.

As soon as God saw that Job's thinking was right, he immediately used him as a minister to help others. He said that his servant Job would pray for his friends because they hadn't spoken that which is right, like his servant Job.

There is nobody like our God. How marvelous is his name! Declare his goodness, get into his arms of protection, and walk the rest of your life in the blessings of a good, forgiving, merciful God of love. God has great things for you. Always trust God. If we trust in God, we will never be ashamed or disappointed.

"Some trust in chariots, and some in horses: but we will remember the name of the LORD our God" (Ps. 20: 7).

"Trust in the LORD, and do good; so shalt thou dwell in the land, and verily thou shalt be fed. Delight thyself also in the LORD; and he shall give thee the desires of thine heart. Commit thy way unto the LORD; trust also in him; and he shall bring it to pass" (Ps. 37: 3–5).

Conclusion

As long as it does not violate his integrity, there is nothing God won't do to deliver us and put us in a place of blessing. It is not his desire for us to be used up and abused by the Enemy. If we are determined to keep our troubles because we have to be right, God will let us, because he has given us a free will.

He lets us make our own decisions, but he is doing everything he can to show us how much he loves us. He continually shows us how wonderful he is to us if we will just trust him.

God has given us apostles, pastors, teachers, evangelists, prophets, and people with wonderful gifts, talents, and abilities to minister to us. He also speaks directly to us in our spirit so that we would run to him and get in that hiding place of God where he protects and provides for us.

Why aren't we always under the shadow of his wing in the hiding place of God? We are doing things our own way with our own way of thinking. We cannot stay under his wing without the full revelation of the goodness of God. A natural son won't climb up in his daddy's lap if he thinks he is going to receive a smack or something bad from his daddy.

Have you ever seen a child nestled without fear in his daddy's arms? Isn't it beautiful? That could be us with our heavenly Father. Receive the revelation that God is always for us. Armed with that knowledge, let's decide to move under the shadow of the Almighty, trusting him. Let's put ourselves in a place where God is in control and we have victory, even if there is a storm blowing.

Remember, there is a difference between what God will cause to happen and what he will allow. God allowed Adam to sin and he will allow us to sin. He will permit us to be sick and broke. He has given us this earth. He has given us his authority. He has given us Holy Ghost power and he has given us the blessing of Abraham. Now, what are we going to do with them? It is not God's will for you to be sick and broke, but he will allow it because you are free.

Even when Job's thinking was all messed up, God called him perfect or mature and upright, and by the end of the book, Job was exactly what God had called him. God did the same thing with Gideon. While Gideon was hiding out, God called him a mighty warrior. Gideon became what God called him. We should be careful what we call our children for they will become what we call them.

We should not assess God merely by what we hear. Instead, we should have our own personal encounter with a good God. Remember that our difficulties are not always the consequences of our wrong behavior. That goes for others as well. We should never judge people because something bad has happened in their life. Their brook may have dried up because of what they have done right in obedience to God.

When we have a need we should run to God, believe, and speak a promise in his Word that will bring victory for us. If we trust God, he will always turn to good what the Devil meant for harm.

Recovery and spoil should be normal for children of the king. The Bible says that the curse causeless shall not come. There is sin in this world, and as a result, there is trouble in this world. If man had never sinned, there would be no problems. Things would be on earth as they are in heaven. That's why difficulties in people's lives are not necessarily the result of their sin. We don't judge others but we are instructed to judge ourselves.

We don't judge God because he really is perfect in all his ways. We don't judge others because we can't see into their hearts as God can. We can't discern their thoughts like God can. We don't know all that they have been through like God does. We do know what we have been through. We do know the motives of our own hearts and the things that we have thought. With the help of the Holy Ghost, we can judge ourselves against the Word of God. When trouble comes, we can judge if we have done right. If change is needed, we can repent and trust God, and we will have deliverance just like Job. We yield to God because we trust him and because we know he is for us and not against us.

If we see someone is in trouble, we should give love and help. That is the way of the kingdom of God. We shouldn't judge others, but help them get back on the right track.

"Brethren, if a man be overtaken in a fault, ye which are spiritual, restore such an one in the spirit of meekness; considering thyself, lest thou also be tempted" (Gal. 6: 1).

We know that God never brings sickness or poverty. We have been redeemed from the curse of the law through the shed blood of the Lord Jesus Christ. The curse of the law is poverty, sickness, and spiritual death. We should not accept what Jesus has redeemed us from. You may have heard that God will put us in a position to use our faith so our faith will grow. This is true, yet God will not afflict. Here is the difference between the afflictions of the Enemy and the exercising of our faith as we're led by the spirit of God: If we are led by God, it's similar to working out with weights and using a spotter—someone who stands close and is ready to grab the bar if we falter. God is our spotter and we can trust him. Let's say we are doing bench presses. God will always put more weight on the bar than what we can lift on our own. He watches over us to make sure we are safe. The reason why some people get into fear is because God is an invisible spotter. If we stay within God's workout routine, we are safe. Because we have a free will, God will let us do our own workout. If we go our own way because we don't trust God, we have broken our hedge of protection.

If we work according to God's plan, we are safe and we get stronger. We push as hard as we can and then God holds the bar. We go as far as we can then God does the rest. He works with us. He helps us place the bar on the stand and we finish successfully. We are stronger than before and it feels good. In fact, even the struggle was kind of an enjoyable experience. Now we can handle even more weight and our faith muscles can handle more for the kingdom of God.

The Devil works in just the opposite way. His goal is to make us weaker not stronger. He might take a dumbbell off the rack and knock us on the head while we are lifting a heavy weight. It's not that hard to distinguish a move of God versus a move of the Devil. But sometimes we just don't know for sure. That's okay, just trust God and call on the name of the Lord.

We must know that God is good. If we think God is doing bad things, we can't believe him for our deliverance. We will be double minded. Like Job, we will turn bitter and finally self-righteous. Remember that God only gives us good things. God won't even move a shadow of a turn from his goodness.

"Every good gift and every perfect gift is from above, and cometh down from the Father of lights, with whom is no variableness, neither shadow of turning" (James 1:17).

If you have received Jesus, then God is in you. The whole kingdom of God is in you. God is in you—he is with you, and he is for you. If God be for you, then who can be against you?

"This then is the message which we have heard of him, and declare unto you, that God is light, and in him is no darkness at all."

1 John 1:5

You are encouraged to write me to ask any questions you may have about salvation, healing, and faith. Please write to me at:

David Hope
Words of Life Church
7811 FM 1960 East
Humble, TX 77346

davidahope@ymail.com

God bless you,

David Hope

What others are saying ......

"*The Goodness of God* is an insightful, balanced and practical book that answers your questions of how God deals in our daily experience. It is jam packed with God's Word and is easy to apply to your life. How we think about God affects how we feel about ourselves and how we treat others. This book gives us an understanding of his love and his desire to bless us. It opens our hearts and minds to be blessed and be a blessing. I wholeheartedly recommend *The Goodness of God*.

Lee Short, Missionary to Mexico/Founder and President of Vida International

Pastor David Hope lives the message he teaches in his book *The Goodness of God*. That message is simply this, God is not double-minded, one day blessing you and the next day cursing you; rather, it is the devil's work that "kills, steals and destroys"; but God-in-Christ has come that we "might have life and have it more abundantly" (Jn 10:10, 1 Jn 3:8). Pastor Hope defends this biblical truth in the face of numerous traditional interpretations of scripture that depict God as the source of our evil circumstances. He does so lucidly and with convincing force. I heartily commend to you *The Goodness of God*.

Bron Barkley, MA, DMIN
Pastor/Missionary Evangelist
Shalom Hebraic Christian Congregation

Good news is always encouraging and uplifting to each of us. David Hope's book, *The Goodness of God*, is packed with good news not just for the hereafter, but for the here and now. If you are going through a storm, this book will bring you hope. If the devil has stolen something from you, this book will give you insight that will cause you rejoice. *The Goodness of God* will edify your spirit man and educate your natural mind to look and receive all the good things God has for you.

Oliver D. Stillwell
Pastor of Dayspring Church in Humble, TX

The Goodness of God is a must read for anyone wanting see God move for their life, family and ministry. I can testify of great changes in my thinking by hearing these principles taught for five years at Words of Life Church from the pulpit by Pastor David Hope. In the last three years my ministry has done more than over the past 14 years. I have gone from being just a preacher to be a Radio/TV station owner, book publisher, missionary and traveling minister. I believe this book will give you the insight to what God wants for your life. That is *The Goodness of God.*

Dr. David Yanez
Director of RevMedia Network, RevMedia Publishing
& David Yanez Ministries

Other books from David Hope

Inhabiting Eternity on Earth

God's Perspective on Money

Do You Want to be Healed?

Jesus of Nazareth, Socialist or Capitalist?

Other Books from RevMedia Publishing

Almost Out of Grace by David Yanez

The Recruit by David Yanez

How to Function in this Economy by Gerald Davis

Simple Gospel by Eric Scott

To order more books of The Goodness of the God or any other of the books on this page. Please visit our website
www.revmediapublishing.com

You can also visit your local bookstore or online book merchant

Prayer for Salvation

Life is not as complicated as most people think. If you are in covenant with Jesus, all you have to do is please him and everything else takes care of itself. Trust in God and make him your source of supply and by faith you can live on earth like it is in heaven.

"Therefore take no thought, saying, What shall we eat? Or, Wherewithal shall we be clothed? (for after all these things do the Gentiles seek) for your heavenly Father knowth that ye have need of all these things. But seek ye first the Kingdom of God and his righteousness; and all these things shall be added unto you."(Mt 6:31-33)

Those that have entered into a blood covenant with God by being born again by the spirit of God have eternal life and can walk in health and prosper.

"Beloved, I wish above all things that thou mayest proper and be in health, even as thy soul prospereth."(3Jn2)

Remember, God does not automatically heal and prosper you. We have to call upon his promises in the name of Jesus. Every good thing comes to us through Jesus. The only qualification to receive from the Father is that we know his Jesus. We have to have made Jesus our Lord and Savior.

Every one needs Jesus because our sins have separated us from a holy God. There is not anyone who has not told a lie or committed a sin. God, however, is holy and cannot fellowship with sin.

So he sent his son, Jesus, to be a man and pay for our sins that we might have the righteousness of God.

Jesus took on our sins and by faith we can receive the exchange of his righteousness and therefore boldly enter into the throne of grace. It's not based on what we have done but what Jesus has done for us. If you will receive Jesus, you will never have to be ashamed again, for Jesus will not be ashamed of you.

"For both he that sanctifieth and they who are sanctified are all of one: for which cause he is not ashamed to call them brethren."(He 2:11)

Because of the sin of Adam, we stand condemned until we receive Jesus by faith. Jesus did not come into the world to condemn the world but to set us free from the condemnation we are already in. It is a free gift of God. We simply receive it by faith.

"Therefore as by the offence of the judgement came upon all men to condemnation: even so by the righteousness of one free gift upon all men unto justification of life. For as by one man's disobedience many were made sinners, so by the obedience of one shall many be made righteous. More over the law entered, that the offence might abound. But where sin abounded, grace did much more abound: That as sin hath reigned unto death, even so might grace reign through righteousness unto eternal life by Jesus Christ our Lord."(Ro 5:18-21)

If you have never received Jesus into your heart but you would like to, then pray this prayer and mean it in your heart. You will inherit eternal life and can begin walking in your inheritance by receiving provision and health on this earth in the name of Jesus.

Lord Jesus, I am a sinner. Forgive me of my sins, come into my heart and make me brand new. Wash me clean in your precious blood. I confess you as my Lord and Savior and I will serve you all the days of my life. Jesus, thank you for saving me and I thank you that I am now a child of God and my name is written in Heaven. I thank you that I now can call upon your name for healing and provision. Help me to make you my source of supply for every area of my life.   AMEN

Prayer for Healing

Jesus wants you healed. All we have to do is ask and believe his word.

"And Jesus departed from thence, and came nigh unto the Sea of Galilee; and went up into a mountain, and sat down there. And great multitudes came unto him, having with them those that were lame, blind, dumb, and many others, and cast them down at Jesus' feet; and he healed them: insomuch that the multitude wondered, when they saw the dumb to speak, the maimed to be whole, the lame to walk, and the blind to see: and they glorified the God of Israel."(Mt 15:29-31)

You see, it's the healing that glorifies God, sickness only glorifies the devil. You can still glorify God when you are sick but God is never glorified in sickness. Great multitudes came to Jesus and he healed them all. To me a multitude of people is as many people as the eye can see. A great multitude of people is more than that. Great multitudes are even more than that. Yet Jesus did not turn even one person away but healed them all.

Some people think that God won't heal them because of some bad things they have done. Healing is for whosoever will receive it by faith. It is not based on performance. Don't you think that in great multitudes that there is at least one person whose performance is worse than yours? Yet, Jesus healed them.

In great multitudes you will find every kind of person. You'll find rich and poor, young and old, and every ethnic background. In great multitudes, there are educated people and those with no schooling, people from good families and people from bad families. There are those that are married, singled and divorced. There are people with religious training and people who have never even prayed before. There are kind people and mean people. There are people who are sexually pure and those that have performed perversion. There are all kinds of people. Jesus healed them all.

God desires greatly for us to receive our healing. Jesus took 39 stripes on his back so that we could be healed. Jesus will never say no to your healing. If Jesus wanted to say no, he wouldn't have had to take one stripe. He didn't take stripes on his back to say no, he took the stripes so that he could say, YES! Pray this prayer out loud and believe God for healing.

Father,

I come to you in the name of Jesus. I give you thanks that by your stripes I was healed and I receive it now by faith. I speak God life and resurrection power into my body to make me whole from the top of my head to the soles of my feet for the glory of God. I release my faith for it and count it as already done in the name of Jesus. Amen.

Please visit us at Words of Life Church....

David Hope is the Senior Pastor of Words of Life Church, a non-denominational, spirit filled, family church located in Humble, Texas. If you're in the Houston/Humble area please join us for service.

Words of Life Church
7811 FM 1960
Humble TX 77346

Service Times:
Sunday Morning 10:40am
Sunday Evening 6:00pm
Wednesday Evening 7:00pm

www.wordsoflifechurch.net

Notes

Notes

Notes

Notes

Notes

Notes

Notes

Notes

Notes

www.ingramcontent.com/pod-product-compliance
Lightning Source LLC
Chambersburg PA
CBHW061650040426
42446CB00010B/1670